Spiritual Power and Integrity

Also by Dr David R. Hawkins

BOOKS

Book of Slides: The Complete Collection Presented at the 2002–2011 Lectures with Clarifications

Discovery of the Presence of God: Devotional Nonduality

The Ego Is Not the Real You: Wisdom to Transcend the Mind and Realize the Self

The Evolution of Consciousness: Navigating the Levels of Awareness and Unlocking Spiritual Potential

The Eye of the I: From Which Nothing Is Hidden

Healing and Recovery

I: Reality and Subjectivity

In the World, But Not of It: Transforming Everyday Experience into a Spiritual Path

The Highest Level of Enlightenment: Transcend the Levels of Consciousness for Total Self-Realization

Letting Go: The Pathway of Surrender

The Map of Consciousness Explained: A Proven Energy Scale to Actualize Your Ultimate Potential

Power vs. Force: The Hidden Determinants of Human Behavior

Reality, Spirituality and Modern Man

Success Is for You: Using Heart-Centered Power Principles for Lasting Abundance and Fulfillment

Transcending the Levels of Consciousness: The Stairway to Enlightenment

Truth vs. Falsehood: How to Tell the Difference

The Wisdom of Dr. David R. Hawkins: Classic Teachings on the Spiritual Truth and Enlightenment

AUDIO PROGRAMMES

How to Surrender to God

Live Life as a Prayer

The Map of Consciousness Explained

All of the above are available at your local bookstore, or may be ordered by visiting:

Hay House UK: www.hayhouse.co.uk
Hay House USA: www.hayhouse.com®
Hay House Australia: www.hayhouse.com.au
Hay House India: www.hayhouse.co.in

Spiritual Power and Integrity

Uncovering Spiritual Reality and Realizing Peace, Love and Divinity

Dr David R. Hawkins

HAY HOUSE
Carlsbad, California • New York City
London • Sydney • New Delhi

Published in the United Kingdom by:
Hay House UK Ltd, 1st Floor, Crawford Corner,
91–93 Baker Street, London W1U 6QQ
Tel: +44 (0)20 3927 7290; www.hayhouse.co.uk

Text © The David and Susan Hawkins Revocable Trust, 2025

Cover design: Julie Davison
Interior design: Karim J. Garcia

The moral rights of the authors have been asserted.

All rights reserved. No part of this book may be reproduced by any mechanical, photographic or electronic process, or in the form of a phonographic recording; nor may it be stored in a retrieval system, transmitted or otherwise be copied for public or private use, other than for 'fair use' as brief quotations embodied in articles and reviews, without prior written permission of the publisher.

The information given in this book should not be treated as a substitute for professional medical advice; always consult a medical practitioner. Any use of information in this book is at the reader's discretion and risk. Neither the authors nor the publisher can be held responsible for any loss, claim or damage arising out of the use, or misuse, of the suggestions made, the failure to take medical advice or for any material on third-party websites.

A catalogue record for this book is available from the British Library.

Tradepaper ISBN: 978-1-83782-212-6
E-book ISBN: 978-1-4019-7713-9

10 9 8 7 6 5 4 3 2 1

This product uses responsibly sourced papers, including recycled materials and materials from other controlled sources. For more information, see www.hayhouse.co.uk

The authorized representative in the EU for product safety and compliance is Penguin Random House Ireland, Morrison Chambers, 32 Nassau Street, Dublin D02 YH68, Ireland. https://eu-contact.penguin.ie

Printed and bound by CPI Group (UK) Ltd, Croydon CR0 4YY

Contents

The Map of Consciousness® vi
Introduction vii

CHAPTER 1:   The Nature of Divinity 1
CHAPTER 2:   Transcending the Intellect
                  through Beauty 21
CHAPTER 3:   How to Reach the High Levels
                  of Consciousness 59
CHAPTER 4:   Transcending the Mind through
                  "No Mind" 81
CHAPTER 5:   The Source of Our Existence Is Silence 123

Conclusion 157
About the Author 159

Map of Consciousness®

God-view	Life-view	Level		Log	Emotion	Process
Self	Is	Enlightenment	⇑	700-1000	Ineffable	Pure Consciousness
All-Being	Perfect	Peace	⇑	600	Bliss	Illumination
One	Complete	Joy	⇑	540	Serenity	Transfiguration
Loving	Benign	Love	⇑	500	Reverence	Revelation
Wise	Meaningful	Reason	⇑	400	Understanding	Abstraction
Merciful	Harmonious	Acceptance	⇑	350	Forgiveness	Transcendence
Inspiring	Hopeful	Willingness	⇑	310	Optimism	Intention
Enabling	Satisfactory	Neutrality	⇑	250	Trust	Release
Permitting	Feasible	Courage	⇕	200	Affirmation	Empowerment
Indifferent	Demanding	Pride	⇓	175	Scorn	Inflation
Vengeful	Antagonistic	Anger	⇓	150	Hate	Aggression
Denying	Disappointing	Desire	⇓	125	Craving	Enslavement
Punitive	Frightening	Fear	⇓	100	Anxiety	Withdrawal
Disdainful	Tragic	Grief	⇓	75	Regret	Despondency
Condemning	Hopeless	Apathy	⇓	50	Despair	Abdication
Vindictive	Evil	Guilt	⇓	30	Blame	Destruction
Despising	Miserable	Shame	⇓	20	Humiliation	Elimination

© The Institute for Spiritual Research, Inc., dba/Veritas Publishing. This chart cannot be reproduced.

Introduction

"What is spiritual truth?" "What or who can I really trust on a spiritual journey?" "Is it possible to live with spiritual intention and still be in the world fulfilling my earthly responsibilities?"

The answers to these questions are yes, and Dr. Hawkins gives solutions and comfort to all spiritual aspirants traveling a pathway of spiritual growth.

In this insightful book, Dr. David R. Hawkins delves more deeply into specific major topics, which can bring greater freedom to anyone interested in spirituality and walking the path toward greater spiritual awareness.

Using the muscle testing method, and stating specific spiritual statements, Dr. Hawkins calibrates many beliefs that mankind has held to be true, but actually have been blocks to our spiritual progress and evolution both individually and collectively.

By shining the light on these misconceptions and presenting the highest truths for our learning, our journey to spiritual advancement can become more straightforward.

In your hands is book 4 of a 6-book series. It comprises the transcribed lectures 7 and 8 presented in July and August 2002 by Dr. Hawkins. We have kept the transcriptions as pure as possible but have deleted redundancies and grammatical inconsistencies.

Some of the topics discussed in this book are:

PART 1:

- Revealing Spiritual Reality by Dispelling Religious/Spiritual Fallacy
- The Importance and Meaning of Context and Content

- How to Surpass the Intellect
- Devotion to Truth Transcends All Obstacles
- The True Nature of God
- Love and Beauty: Qualities of Divinity

PART 2:

- Understanding the Ego Disassembles It
- Causality Is an Illusion
- Knowingness and Transformation
- What Is Advaita?: The Pathway of Nonduality
- "No Mind" Is Silent
- Spiritual Power and Intention

After reading this book, our wish for you is greater higher awareness and stronger motivation that impels you on your journey of awakening.

Susan Hawkins and the Veritas Staff

CHAPTER 1

The Nature of Divinity

Today we're representing our rights. We're declaring the rights of God and protecting God's good name. And we're here in the name of protecting the good name of God today, who has been much maligned over the thousands of years, blamed for everything—catastrophes, earthquakes, floods, drought—and because of God, we can't picnic in the woods around Sedona right now; there's a drought. It never dawned on primitive man that—you know, the sort of makers of ancient gods—that these things went on before mankind existed. The time to blame God for human catastrophe—when humans weren't even here yet, and earthquakes were going on, and floods and fires were going on, so, it strikes—you know, the pre-Christian history was where it began, and conceptions of God were pretty much anthropomorphic, in which God takes the blame for everything: sort of a dualistic perception of God which persists to this common day and still causes consternation.

The next book we're doing, we're calibrating the energies of the greatest theologians of history and what the level of truth is of all the religions, branches of religions, spiritual groups, teachers, historical scriptures, et cetera. And if I'm still living, it'll be published in a year or two.

Well, when you talk about the absolute truth of God, you can see that you jeopardize a great deal on this planet, whose survival is based on not on the truth of God, but on the *falsification* of the truth of God. That's their power base, their financial base; gets them the publicity, gets those bucks from all you listeners out there in TV land.

From some of the questions we get in the mail, people think that Susan and I make these things up, that what we find is whatever we believe.

The kinesiologic method of ascertaining truth, of differentiating truth from falsehood, arose from over 20 years of research. Over the years, I would have groups, and all of us did kinesiology at once. And we did this all over the world many, many times.

But those who have not witnessed any of those things—and I thought, today we'll do something like we did over the years, and we'll do it with this group here. And these are statements that are going into the new book, and we're going to check them out and make sure they're true before we put them in there, okay? This is sort of a rattle-bone, rattly-bone statement of spiritual reality, and it's going to shake up people, and we want to make sure that we're not lying. God really is awful, you oughtta be scared of him, you know what I mean? That did come up this morning, didn't it? Um-hum. That came up this morning. Suddenly I felt a huge shock of, like, an attack of immense fear coming up. Wow! It was a big one and coming up from the collective unconscious.

So, today, we want to demonstrate how we verify these things. They come from this consciousness as a knowingness, and then to express it in the world takes languaging, expression in literary form, and so we verify the truth of the statement. Or not, see?

So, that came up today. "What I felt was tremendous fear: resist." [True.] "It came up from the collective unconscious: resist." [True.] "It came up as the totality of the error of the misunderstanding of God: resist." [True.] "The unconscious fear of the apocalypse is what we cleared this morning: resist." [True.] Yeah. You don't think that was a strong one—it came up, like, *whoosh*—incumbent in the human psyche for 2,000 years. It had a lot of energy.

Let's see what happened to the consciousness of mankind. "The consciousness of mankind was over 207." [True.] "Now is over 208." [True.] "209." [True.] "210." [Not true.] "Now over 209." [True.] "209.5." [Not true.] "209." Oh, I thought I'd squeeze an extra half a point. That means somebody out there's not paying attention, or I'd have a point. You'd better wake up.

Also, when you make declarations of truth, that always brings up that which is untrue; it triggers it up for examination and verification.

As we see in the book *I: Reality and Subjectivity*—the reason I'm talking about it is because I'm just finishing this book in which we sort of trace the evolution of creation, the dawning of the light of God as consciousness, the evolution of that consciousness throughout all of time and throughout all of time on this planet—its evolution through the various life-forms, which takes us through all the theories of evolution and creation, which we pretty much settled with this crowd before, that evolution and creation are one and the same thing.

"What we affirm at each lecture is the absolute reality that all things are what they are by virtue of the Divinity of their creation, which is continuous; and it is the presence of God that accounts for all existence at every instant: resist." [True.]

You know, this is the first time in history there's really been any kind of valid spiritual research. Is that a fact? That's a fact. There's never been a tool to really do spiritual research. There's been historical research in which you crawl through the deserts looking for old scriptures and deciphering the undecipherable: what you find on the sides of tombs and various hidden places. Or you find relics, or you find bones, or you find the validation that such and such a community did live a thousand years ago. That's archaeologic, that's history and research. That has nothing to do with spiritual reality.

Theology is the study of the nature of religion as it evolved over the millennia and of course is an extremely interesting subject in and of itself. I could easily have become a theologian. I got straight As in theology at a Jesuit university; that should get you in the door, right? At the time, I was an atheist, but that didn't bother my understanding of theology. And I respect theology, and you can define the limit of theology. So, we don't want to stress theology beyond which it is equipped to go, because theology and science are somewhat similar in that they're both in the 400s. And once you get up to about 496 or 498, you can't go farther with it. You can't really go farther with science or theology, because that's as far as the intellect will take you.

I read a very erudite paper on the relationship of consciousness and advanced theoretical physics, quantum theory. The only difficulty is, science can only take you to the high 400s, and the realities—spiritual realities really don't show up with any strong indication until you get into the 500s, so there's a block, and as I read this paper, it's extremely erudite; it's beyond my capacity to comprehend the mathematics of quantum mechanics. But what I got, the feeling I got, was that the intellect is being pushed to the almost painful limit of where it can go, you know. And I've read a number of those things, and I hear them at science-and-consciousness kinds of conferences. You always come up with the same answer to that which is not comprehensible. So, the difficulty with science and advanced theoretical physics is, it takes us right to the door, and what we've suspected and what we've said before is that quantum potentiality *is* the doorway. "That infinite quantum potentiality is the infinite doorway of infinite potentiality: resist." [True.]

Yes, so we're correct. That *is* the doorway. Except with science, you can't go through the doorway. So, what science does is take us up, and this is very erudite and very impressive, and always makes me want to go back to school and study quantum mechanics and math. I like quantum mechanics; I don't like the math that goes with it. But it does take you right up to the door. But it doesn't take you *through* the door. To get through the door, you've got to jump, even Einstein. Einstein's 499. You have to jump through to the 500s. And so, the intellect takes you as far as it can go.

I respect theology because I find it very fascinating, and I really could spend a couple of years just going to a theological seminary. I'd just love doing that. So, if I had another lifetime or two, I would just blow a whole one just going to a theological seminary and writing up theological treatises.

* * *

So, I thought we would start with, then, discussing the reality of God and try and nail it down. I mean, nobody has ever nailed it down, much less publicly. There's exhortations. I watch some of these preachers; they're wonderful, they're dramatic—they have great dramatic ability, and they're very impassioned. And if I were a follower of theirs, I'd probably be a very enthusiastic follower.

So, how can we verify, then, what has been bandied about? See, if you look up *theology* in *Encyclopedia Britannica*, it runs quite a few pages. I mean, a lot of theologians—a lot has been said, going back to ancient Greece. And it takes you into philosophy and metaphysics, and, of course, the crux of it is epistemology. So, those of you who are intellectuals know that the crux of theology, then, really ends up in the hard problems of epistemology, and epistemology can only take you to the door. Epistemology can only take you to the door. Epistemology can only take you—the truth of epistemology can only take you to 499. "That's correct: resist." [True.] Yeah, it does. It only takes you to 499. Why is that? Because you're still in "mind." And "mind," intrinsically, in order to be "mind," has to be dualistic. So, the reason theology, epistemology, philosophy, advanced theoretical physics, quantum mechanics can't take you through the door is because they're all dualistic systems of knowingness. They're all dualistic; there's a "this" and a "that"; there's a "me" and a—there's the self and that which is known, and which is different than the Self.

So, all of these will take us right to the door, but they won't take us through the door. Some other quality is required. I think a study of theology gives you great respect for the human intellect. I mean, the way God transcendent versus God immanent is discussed in all the various world religions is quite impressive. I find it quite fascinating. But what you're really understanding through this study is how the human mind works. What you end up with as a straight-A student in theology, epistemology, advanced theoretical physics, and quantum mechanics is an extremely advanced and sophisticated understanding of how the human mind works. That's where it takes you: right to the door. However, that drive that takes a person to the door, I think, if correctly recontextualized, has the power to take you through the door. Anybody who spends their whole life getting right up to the door—"Knock, knock. Anybody home? Is there a God?" Anybody who spends their whole life straining to get there has certainly got enough momentum and motivation to break through the door. And it only requires unblocking, unblocking that door.

So today, I thought, we'll make some statements about God and see if they're verifiable, and I thought we might even do kinesiology. You see, kinesiology itself calibrates at 600. Kinesiology is at the doorway between the ego and the nonego, between the duality and nonduality. So, it stands like a guardian at the door. Kinesiology itself, as a science, calibrates with reliability. "Kinesiology itself calibrates exactly at 600: resist." [True.] Wow, 600 is exactly where you shift from ego into enlightenment, so it's a critical level.

Therefore, kinesiology is difficult. People try to grasp it intellectually. I say, "Don't try to grasp it intellectually. When you stab yourself, it bleeds—that's good enough, isn't it? When you stand in the sun, in the sun you get warm. When you stand in the rain, you get wet. That's all you have got to know about it. If you ask—the most futile question to ask about anything is *why*, because the ultimate reality, there is no why. There is no why. Therefore, all these are based on a fallacy. The first fallacy is that of duality, which is built into languaging and logic and conceptualization itself.

Therefore, to derive a truth is totally subjective. So, what logic and all these things we're looking for is, by means of duality, to try and discover the nature of that which is nondualistic. It can't be done. There's a chapter I'm writing called "The Final Blocks to the Doorway," because at the doorway at 600, when you walk through, you can't take duality with you. You cannot take any baggage with you. All that you've ever known, think, believe in, can mentalize about, conceptualize about, you cannot take with you. It has to be left at the door, because at that point, mind disappears. You can't take the content of mind with you when the mind disappears; it dissolves with the mind. So, all of that you have accumulated is, at that point, useless. It's useful to get to the door, but then at that door, one has to drop it.

* * *

Despite the disagreements over the centuries about sacred scriptures of various religions, collectively there is a verifiable, authentic source of man's knowledge of the nature of Divinity, which is actually quite impressive in their unanimity and concordance. There emerges, then, a substratum of irreducible truth, verified in all cultures throughout all times by those that we call mystics, sages. We now have recently discovered a calibration technique verifying truth from falsehood so as to be able to reaffirm spiritual reality and end up with sort of a modern-day theology, which, we will call this new religion *Spirituality*. Spirituality is that religious discipline in which that which is provably the truth has been extracted historically, subjectively, and experimentally, see, because the source of all my own knowledge is all three, the states that appeared of their own accord; then later on, studying and finding a way of objective verification; and then we see the subjective, the radical subjectivity of people who've experienced the presence of God has been exactly the same throughout all cultures, throughout all histories, throughout all millennia. It's always been the same. Therefore, anything that varies from that requires explanation instead of the other way around. Well, traditional religion puts it the other way around. Scripture is what is the authority, and the mystic had better be beaten and burned until they change their mind and come around to the truth as the truth saw it.

There is therefore available, by a sophisticated intellect subjectively, objectively, historically, a core of absolute validity that transcends all positionalities—and all positionalities are maneuverings for advantage or gain. The only reason you can believe the mystic is because there is no advantage or gain to it. All things are suspect if there's gain or advantage. Inasmuch as one has all there is to have, knows all there is to know, and is all what is possible to be, there's hardly any gain the world can dangle in front of you. Like, what already?

So, we're going to start out and we'll verify these statements, which will now become the famous "Sedona Declaration" in defense of the good name of God. I'll read the first one, and we're going to ask if whether this is the truth or not.

We're going to make irreducible statements about the essential nature of God as my own understanding and experience, as well as theologically verifiable. These are going to be statements in which we're going to settle it for mankind forever, okay?

First statement: "God is both manifest as the totality and allness of creation, and unmanifest as the Godhead, the infinite potentiality and source, quote, in parenthesis, '(voidness),' prior to form." "That is a fact: resist." [True.] "That is absolute truth." [True.] "The level of that truth is over 900." [True.] "980." [True.] "999." [True.] "1000." [Not true.] That is the absolute truth to the degree that it's knowable in mankind.

Statement number two: "God is infinite beyond time, space, locality, and without beginning or end: resist; that's true. [True.] "The level of truth is 1000: resist." [True.] Thank you. Without beginning or end, see what I mean? God is—these are commonly stated theology, but we will prove it for ourselves. "God is omnipresent." "God is omnipresent." "God is the same as Allness, Omnipotent, and Omniscient: resist." Those statements are verifiably true. They don't depend on anybody's opinion. "God is the source and substrate of consciousness, awareness, knowingness, and sentience: resist."

Now, this is very interesting, having to do with science. "God is the sole source of life: resist." [True.] "God is the sole source of the energy of life: resist." [True.] See, creation comes from the top down, but evolution goes from the bottom up. So, life can appear as a worm.

Now let's test this out. Sometimes what we do, we test all these—see, you have to have internal consistency. If this is true, then we will test its opposite. "Life arose accidentally as a spontaneous interaction of chemistry: resist." [Not true.] There goes science—goodbye. Goodbye, science as a source of life. We're going to just confirm this—evolution: "We have permission to ask this." [True.] "Evolution occurs within consciousness, which then manifests as form: resist." [True.] Yeah. See, the reason there's a missing link—because there isn't any missing link in form, you see, because creation is continuous. Each billiard ball is continuously created to be what it is. What we see is the branching of a branch, but the evolution of consciousness, the evolution of the species occurs on the invisible level of the domain of consciousness. That's where the shift in the evolution of form, because you see, the form includes aesthetics. When you just think how the eye works, you see, it just didn't accidentally learn how to blink on itself. I mean, who the heck would have thought of that? You know what I mean? "Consciousness saw that construction, and by holding it in mind, it manifests as an eye: resist." [True.] So, the eye didn't just go up accidentally, you see. That's enough science for today.

"God is the source of evolution and creation, which are identical and ever continuous and ongoing into this moment: resist." [True.] Yeah. What does creation look like? Creation looks like a roomful of people testing each other with kinesiology, don't you see? The unfolding of everybody is becoming, fulfilling the potentiality of their own essence. That's all that's happening: "God is the source and essence of peace, love, stillness, and beauty: resist." [True.]

We're going to have fun when we get through with this serious list: "God is beyond all universes, all materiality, all galaxies, and yet the source of all that is: resist." [True.] Okay. See, when you see God as "source" rather than "cause," you have a whole different ballgame of theology. Take that back to Michigan! The reason theology gets stuck in epistemology, and the reason advanced theoretical physics gets stuck, is because this is still seeing things in terms of causality. Causality is a dualistic deception; there's a "this" causing a "that." There's no "this" causing a "that." The essence of that which is the source of all existence opens itself like this. It's really revealing the truth of that which it is. Nothing is causing anything. As the rose unfolds, nothing is *causing* it to unfold. The form is dependent on prevailing conditions: sunlight, water, et cetera. But it is not the sunlight and all that's causing the flower to unfold. The essence of the flower is intrinsic to its creation, and it's merely revealing to you that which it is, because that's how creation manifests itself in that which we perceive as the present reality. [Testing:] "That truth is 1000: resist." [True.] What was just spoken is the absolute truth.

"God is the sole source of existence, and the potentiality of beingness is true: resist." "God is the ultimate context of which the universe and all that exists is the content: resist." [True.]

"Out of the Unmanifest arises the manifest expressing itself as the entire universe, and of course, all the universes are without end, because everything that is created by the Creator contains the same essence as the Creator. Consequently, each universe that is created out of the fact that that is innate to its own essence is creating an infinite series of infinite universes which are creating infinite universes, which are creating infinite universes because that is their essence." "That's true: resist." [True.] Whoa, boggled myself there a second.

So, it's critically different in theology to understand the difference between "cause" and "source." You see the error in the classic, uh, theologian—who's the basic, classic theologian in Catholicism? Thomas Aquinas. You see, well, Aristotle also did the same thing. When you go back through an endless series of causes, you're looking for the primary cause. There's the error: to think that the primary in a series is the same as the sequence of the series. The source of the series is not the same as the series; it's of a different class. In fact, it's a category logic error to presume that there's one big billiard ball that created all the rest of the billiard balls in the universe. What makes the first billiard ball move is a non-billiard ball. Wow. Right. So, trying to find God—call God as the primary cause of all causes, then, is a logic error, made by Aristotle and made by most theologians since. The beginning of a series is something that is *not* of that series. You got that reality? For this to exist, something that it is *not* is the beginning of the series. So, in looking for the primary cause, you don't look for a cause. You look instead for the source. The source requires no explanation, because it's not an endless series of causes. Oh, I'm knocking myself out this morning. What is this? It's because I have to read my own writing, and it's on yellow paper, of all things.

"God is the a priori, a priori formless Source of existence within all form: resist." [True.]

"Within the illusion of form is nonform, which is the essence of form. Without nonform, no form could exist. That's true: resist." [True.] "God is not within the preview of the provable or the intellect: resist." [True.] "That which is provable by the intellect to reason could, by definition, not be God: resist." [True.] The God that you can prove by the intellect, then, cannot possibly be God, because that which is beyond the intellect is not provable by the intellect. So, all you could prove by the intellect is the *concept* of God. That, you can prove with the intellect. For God to be God, it would have to meet certain requirements. So, you can prove the intellectual position about God, but that has nothing to do with the existence of God. Okay.

"God is the Source and essence of the subjective state of 'I-ness' called Enlightenment: resist." [True.] So, what the spiritual student is looking for, then, is God Immanent, God as the Self with capital S. God as the essence out of which one's own existence is continuously arising. It didn't arise 75 years ago. It's arising right this moment. My birth is happening continuously. My existence is continuously sustained, just like a water fountain holds up a rubber ball, see. It's being held up continuously. It isn't the water that came out of this faucet eight minutes ago that's holding up the ball; it's the presence of God *now* that is holding up the ball on top of the fountain. The minute you shut off the fountain, the ball drops. O Lord, amen, I scared myself there. That's why we call it *The Eye of the I*—because you're really talking about the third eye of the Buddhic body, the third eye of the Atmic body, the realization of the "I" as, uh, anyway. [Testing:] "God is the radical subjectivity of Self-realization with a capital S: resist." [True.] So, this is the way of, we're going to talk about the way through the heart, maybe in the lecture after next if I can get through that lecture. Now we're preparing the way.

God is the radical subjectivity, so the realization of the Self is a radically subjective state. That's why it's difficult to see. We're so used to space being around us, we don't notice space. When you walk into the room, you notice all these objects. If I ask you how much space was there, you'd say: "What space? There isn't any space there."

Nobody notices the space, because we take for granted the presence of the Self without really realizing its true nature. "God is descriptively both immanent and transcendent, and those two terms are merely artifacts of vocabulary: resist." [True.] There's not two different Gods, immanent and transcendent. Well, you think that sounds trivial. This is a sophisticated audience, and this would seem obvious to you, but there's a lot of great world religions; there isn't a God immanent and a God transcendent. So, we can't say God is both, because to say both is already the same logical error. Okay.

"The human experience of the presence of God is the same in all ages, all cultures, all localities: resist." [True.] The experience of the presence of God is absolutely the same in everyone." You go back to the ancient Aryan sages; their description is the same. See, the reason why I nailed this down is because anybody, anything that varies from this is going to have to explain themself. We'll put them through the inquisition; we have our own little rack. God is immanent and transcendent! Okay, thank you! "The effect on human consciousness of the experience of the presence of God is subjectively transformative and identical throughout human history and is verifiable in the present time by a calibration technique of level of consciousness: resist." [True.] That's what brought up the negative energy this morning when we really got hit by it.

Truth, then, to claim itself as truth, has to withstand the test of truth, huh? If you tell me it floats, I'm going to put it in water. If it sinks to the bottom, I want my money back.

Now listen carefully. Here's a long one: "The essence of God does NOT include human frailties such as partiality, controllingness, duality, judgmentalism, vindictive retaliation, wrath, righteous anger, resentment, vanity, limitation, arbitrariness, revenge, jealousy, vulnerability, or locality. That is a 100 percent correct statement: resist." [True.] That puts us at variance of a couple thousand years of religious tradition, doesn't it? Let's do it one by one. "The essence of God does not include the human frailties such as partiality: resist." [True.] "Partialities are a frailty of the human ego: resist." [True.] For God to have partiality, he couldn't be God; he'd have to be, uh, sort of dumb. "God is not—the essence of God does not include judgmentalism: resist." [True.] "Wrath." [True.] "Righteous anger." [True.] "Vanity." [True.] "Limitation." [True.] "Partiality." [True.] "Location." [True.] And, "Ethnic favoritism: resist." [True.] "God has no favorite geography: resist." [True.] No holy lands.

"The variabilities of the depictions of Divinity reflect the variabilities of human perception and the human ego: resist." [True.] "When the obstacles of human mentation, emotionality, and the ego structure from which they arise are transcended, the Self with a capital S as God Immanent, the Divinity within, shines forth as the essence of one's own sense of 'I,' the Self, capital S: resist." [True.] "The Self shines forth just as the sun shines forth when the clouds are removed: resist." [True.] Okay. "God is the context and source of the karmic unity of all of creation: resist." [True.]

"Therefore, the way to God is really, huh ... through the affirmation of truth, and not to be distracted by these side avenues"—um, because what came up came out of the collective unconscious. "That was the collective unconscious of the totality of the fear of God in mankind: resist." [True.] It was like a ferocious fire going through the nervous system, and I intuited, "Wow, that's what we brought up this morning." Because this lecture, what we're challenging is—you can see what we're challenging, correct? Um-hum. And the tenacious hold it has within the history of mankind.

"The reality of the truth of the nature of God has remained the same throughout all ages and all cultures." It's always been described the same. Therefore, any variations from it would have to require some explanation in understanding, and with kinesiology we've tracked down the sources of the error—you know, historically in many different cultures and various times, and the thing about doing spiritual research is, you come up with astonishing discoveries that nobody discovered before. Why? Because it's never been done before. This is the first time a telescope has been pointed at the heavens, and we discovered there's galaxies out there, and all kinds of astonishing things. "I'm holding in mind a question: resist." "Permissible: resist." [Not true.] Uh-oh. "I'm holding in mind a statement: resist." [True.] "It's permissible to demonstrate in front of this audience: resist." [Not true.] Oh. Wow. We'll find out that one later. Anyway, sometimes we find out astonishing things; then it says, "No, not yet." I don't know why. I guess other information has to be provided first.

DEVOTION TO THE TRUTH TRANSCENDS ALL OBSTACLES

So, this lecture has been sort of sequential preparation of an understanding, a way of approaching spiritual reality, a way of approaching spiritual work, a way of transcending the ego by understanding its nature and not by attacking it. And people are always asking in letters, you know, "How can I advance myself spiritually?" And the basic essence of it is always the same, and that is one's devotion to the truth. One's devotion to the truth transcends all obstacles. Let's see if that's a fact: "That's a fact: resist." [True.] One's devotion to the truth then overcomes all obstacles. And sometimes people will write a letter also that they don't understand certain things, and because there's such a huge volume of letters, they can't all be answered. And so, what we generally say, then, in a letter, that almost—over 90 percent of the questions that are being presented resolve themselves with a little further reflection of the information that's been provided. It takes a certain amount of time to grow, you know what I'm saying? And a lot of times, people will come up with a question that, you know, took me 20 years of meditation to even get to the edge of that answer, and he wants it tomorrow, you know. I say, "Well, now . . ." Hmmm. So, there's a certain maturity, a certain . . . in other words, the growth factor— you know, the growth factor—and each person evolves at their own rate of development. And that rate of development is absolutely correct for that person. And that's why we got the *no*: resist. "That's why we got the *no*: resist." Thank you. Okay. "Some individuals in the group could handle it." "Forty percent could handle it." [True.] "Fifty percent." [True.] "Sixty percent." Okay.

So, therefore some preparation of spiritually advanced work has to be done to become an intense spiritual aspirant. There's a certain level at which the desire to reach the ultimate state is like a driving force that takes over everything. At that point you leave, much to the consternation of the world, everything, and they think you've lost your mind; and hopefully you have, and it takes some years to recover. Some never recover, but anyway. It's not comprehensible to the ordinary person what could have happened to you that made such a difference. Even such a thing as an out-of-body experience is not comprehensible to a lot of people, or near-death experience; those flashes of stillness when you suddenly feel the Presence are not comprehensible to the intellect. The state that came on at age 36 or 37, I forget what it was, there was no one to speak to about it for 30 years. Who are you going to talk to about it? Nobody.

So, these states which are inwardly private become validated by reading about them, knowing about them, hearing other people speak of them. I think each one of us, when we share our own spiritual experience, strengthens that of others that we share a collective strength, and in that sharingness of strength and experience reaffirms. Why does it work that way? Because we live in a world in which all such experience is negated. It's negated, and the validity of it is in question intrinsic to the nature of language itself, intrinsic to the language of nature of science and logic. Right now, the god of our culture is science. In ancient days, man looked to religion for answers, looked to God for answers. Looked to God for salvation. After many centuries of studying the sort of gods of negativity and not getting too far with it and going through the Inquisition and various other tough times, mankind now looks to science, looks to the future, because logic says most of "religiosity" is based on the history of certain individuals' experiences thousands of years ago, or perhaps reinforced by, in the last decades, as reaffirmations. But it very often ends up as a great emphasis on the irrelevant—you know, like the Buddha said, "Make no images of me." And the Buddha is, of course, the most frequently created image on the planet. There's more Buddhas sold than any other image or statue of anything.

So, there's a great deal of emphasis on history, location, things that are really tribal, ethnic, cultural peculiarities then becoming included in these religions and now become part of sacred scripture and religious practice to the point that it eclipses the truth out of which it ostensibly originally arose. You know—whether you wear a turban or you don't wear a turban, what the hell has that got to do with the presence of God in the absolute reality, of infinite reality? I don't know. In other words, that which is totally irrelevant to the reality of God and the presence of God as the truth within yourself is the point of emphasis. The whole point of emphasis now is whether you wear a turban or you don't wear a turban, you know what I mean?

You eat meat on Fridays, whether you eat fish on Fridays. I grew up dreading to eat meat by mistake on a Friday. What if I ate a hamburger and suddenly realize, God, it's Friday! High Episcopal, which is like Catholic, you know. Anyway, in those days, all such things, you know, you forgot a day of obligation—holy mackerel, you know what I mean. And I already related to you the dreadfulness of confession on Saturday afternoon, and I would go for confession, for those who haven't heard, as late as possible on Saturday afternoon, because you weren't supposed to sin between confession and having Communion, Holy Communion. So, the trick was, you arranged to go for confession—you know, "Father, I have sinned, et cetera," as late as possible on Saturday, and you go to the earliest Mass you can get to on Saturday, and, quick, have Communion. And now if you sin, it's not going to be so bad. I mean, you made it, you made it. And I told you the dreadful morning on the way to church, and it was probably 1930-something or other. And here was this giant billboard with a Jantzen swimming-suit ad, and here's this voluptuous blonde in this swimming suit, and the sinful thought began knocking at age 12, you know what I'm talking about? Testosterone raging through your bloodstream. And there's this 32-foot-long lady, and I'm on my way to Communion. Life was a nightmare, I'll tell you. Christianity in the '30s was scary, you know. It's no wonder I became an atheist; I mean, any sensible, intelligent person would become an atheist, and that's what I did. Just the constant fear of guilt. It isn't—you know, it isn't just guilt; it's the fear of guilt, you know. And many people, as they get more spiritually evolved, they're, you know, they're not really afraid of consequences. They're afraid of things out there. They're afraid of their own inner reaction to it: "If I know this, I'm going to be hung with guilt." You know what I'm saying? Shall I steal the pen from the bank or not? Well, if I do, I'm gonna be stuck with guilt. Every time I look at the pen, I'm going to feel a pang of guilt. It's not worth the guilt, huh? Then you become—inwardly, you become your own guru within. When you don't steal a pen because you're afraid of your own sense of guilt that would arise as a result, you are on your way. You are responsible for yourself morally, ethically, and spiritually. And you've reached integrity, because integrity is always not blaming it on something "out there." Once you cross over integrity, calibrated level of 200, now you own a responsibility and you begin to see the source of guilt is going to arise out of yourself, not because there's a spot on your soul and God is going to punish you. So, between late Saturday afternoon and Sunday morning, there was a fear that this sin would appear, and was explained by the preacher that it would appear as a spot on your soul, so I walked around dreading this invisible soul where all these spots would be appearing. And God spotting all these black spots on your soul as you walk by, you know, and of course, that would lead to a fear of Judgment Day and a fearful God of traditional religion, which everyone fears until they realize the true nature of God.

* * *

I think we might do some questions on it, because some people who are doing kinesiology had some questions. One interesting question was: How do you get through the door of the 500s? And that is actually a chapter that I have been writing on. And it has to do with: How do you transcend the experience of reality without deciphering, without channeling it through the intellect? Reason will only take you so far, and then lovingness, devotion, reverence lead to an inner revelation. And traditionally, the methods of doing that, the way of doing it has been prayer, devotion, meditation; umm, the appreciation of beauty.

When I traveled in Europe, I traveled from one cathedral to the other. And go from Westminster Abbey to Chartres to Notre Dame. So, the trip to Europe is from one cathedral to the other. People say, "Why do plan your trip to Europe based on the cathedrals?" Because that, to me, is the epitome of their civilization. Great cathedrals all calibrate around 700. When you walk into Chartres and the choir's practicing at the same time, it's difficult to keep walking, because you almost swoon with beauty. You turn around, and you look at the blue window. The Chartres blue is a very famous blue; it's never been duplicated, and it's so exquisitely beautiful that you almost go weak with it. So, that's one way to transcend to 500 from the 400s . . . is the pursuit of beauty. The chanting of that—let's calibrate it; I didn't calibrate that: "I have permission to calibrate that." [True.] "Om Namaha Shivaya" is over 500." [True.] "550." [True.] "560." [True.] "570." [True.] "580." [True.] "590." [True.] "600." [True.] "Ohmm, over 650." [True.] "Over 680." [True.] "Om Namah Shivaya Ohmmm, over 700." [True.] "Ohmmm over 740." [True.] "Ohmmmm over 760." [True.] "Ohmmm over 780." [True.] "Ohmmm over 790." [True.] "This ohm is over 800." [True] "Ohm over 800." [True.] "Ohm over 850." [Not true.] "Om Namah Shivaya." [True.] "Om Namah Shivaya." [True.] Om Namah.

There's another way over 500. Ohmmm. Let's all do an ohm. We'll get the calibration of this ohm. "It's over 600." [True.] "650." [True.] "700." [True.] "720." [True.] "740." [True.] "760." [Not true.] "This ohm is over 750." [True.] "760." [Not true.] That ohm is 750. So that's the experience of what 750 is like.

You're walking through the woods by yourself, and suddenly time comes to a stop. The incredible beauty of everything shines forth. You look at everything; everything is absolute, incredible beauty. It happens in the high 500s too and makes it very hard to function, because you're always breaking out in tears. In the high 500s, it's difficult to function in the world. The crying-ness of the saint. People who live in monasteries, it's traditional. At a certain stage, it's hard to stop. You cry for a couple of years. I cried for several years. It was impossible. I'd be in an airport, a couple would sit there and look at each other with a glance of love, and it was just—if they weren't loving, it was okay; I could make it. She looks at him with that look, and wow, I'm gone. Incredible beauty does the same thing, right? We've all been in a symphony, a concert, or somebody like Puccini. When Mimi's dying in Puccini, *La bohème*, all of a sudden there's a silence, and then suddenly the orchestra comes in with a chime, like that, and he realizes—"Mimi!" he sings out. And shoosh, it just goes out. What is that note in Puccini? Over 500? So, I still cry at *La bohème*. I've seen *La bohème* many times. But when he realizes—Marcello, or whatever his name is—realizes that Mimi has just died, then you hear, like, the soaring of the soul as it soars . . . and, uh, so we'll stop talking about that. The voice won't continue.

So, the incredible beauty shines forth. And we have a lecture after this one on devotion; how we're going to get through that, I have no idea, because this kind of thing happens all the time. The presence of beauty, hmm, devotion to that beauty. . . . What then becomes revealed is the Divinity, that exquisite perfection of the presence of God manifesting, and now you're allowed to see that beauty. Beauty is different than pretty. The revelation is that the essence of beauty itself, the perfection, the radiance, the energy of beauty, is your awareness; it is your awareness of the presence of God within all that exists. As that becomes permanent, you see it everywhere. You walk down an alleyway in the city of New York, which the world would see in a very derogatory manner, and it looks like a painting by a French impressionist. Here's the garbage can, and here's the dead rat, and here's the tangled mess of so-and-so, and it's just incredibly beautiful. It's like a canvas, a perfect canvas in which the intrinsic beauty of everything shines forth, because there is no superimposition of intellectualism—goodness, badness, ideas of beauty and aversions. So, beauty, because beauty is inherent in everything. . . .

And in the book I'm finishing, I talk about Kleenex Zen and seeing the beauty of when you—when you go in the bathroom and you see a piece of Kleenex sitting there and it suddenly strikes you, its incredible beauty, you know you're getting there. The first time it happened to me, it was in an airplane. And you're sitting there doing your business and you're looking, and here's this Kleenex, and it's like this incredible—I've described it before like a Georgia O'Keeffe painting—the sheer essence of beauty in all that exists.

So, the other doorway past the intellect is aesthetics, the appreciation, the reverence for beauty, the reverence for purity and beauty-ness, and to see the sacredness of all that exists. Because all that exists is coming out of its source, then Divinity is intrinsic in all that exists. The capacity to experience this Divinity directly, and then it becomes relatively innate to one's experience of life itself.

CHAPTER 2

Transcending the Intellect through Beauty

So, how to transcend the intellect? You can't get there via advanced theoretical physics, you can't get there.... You can certainly demonstrate its reality, because using a calibration technique which we talk about, you can calibrate what is the level of that beauty, and we just did it. Its quality is ineffable. We use the term *beauty*—we use the term, but that isn't the quality. What makes your hair stand up on the back of your head when the violin hits a certain note is a different quality of consciousness, and it transcends the intellect.

So, the traditional ways to God, the upside, the positive side of religion has been its recognition of beauty as a great transporter of the human spirit. That's why, to me, the great cathedrals of the world, the great cathedrals of Europe especially, depict probably the greatest possible achievement of mankind within the physical domain. The endless lifetimes—some of those cathedrals took a thousand years to build. Century after century, people devoting their entire life just carving one pulpit in 3-D. And I looked at pulpits. The man spent his entire life—there's three levels of figures within this pulpit—one entire lifetime just to do that one carving. So, we won't talk anymore about beauty. So, that is one of the great and traditional ways to experience what you might say are various aspects of the Presence: that which is love, that which is peace, that which is beauty. Not beauty of perception, not beauty of artistic appreciation, but an awareness that one is experiencing the essence out of which that beauty is being perceived.

So, traditional religion has understood that. So, on the one side, there is the depiction of God as sort of a frightening monster. On the other hand, there is all that really sustains the core and keeps it going, because if there weren't any truth there, it would collapse out of its own negativity.

As you walk into a great cathedral.... One time I was in Cusco, and I wasn't used to the altitude. And as I got off the plane, I got sort of a stoned feeling, you know what I mean? Like everything was incredibly beautiful. As I walked down the street, I could smell this incense. Wow! Incredible. And so, I followed the incense. The stoned feeling was due to the spiritual condition that I arrived at. I arrived in Cusco, and anyway, the odor of the incense was coming down the street, and so I automatically followed this incense to where it was coming from, and it was coming from an ancient church. The church had all these altars, and these altars were all made of heavy silver, and you could see the prior influence on it. Anyway, it was right before Christmas, and as you got into the church, the incense got heavier and heavier, and the organ was playing flute music, Peruvian flute music, a type of religious music that played on—it was coming with the sound of Indian flutes. So, here's this incredible flute music, and the incense wafting through the air, and it's coming out of a great, big kiln—up near the front of the altar is this big, black thing, and this incense is pouring out. There's stained-glass windows, and the sunshine is coming through the stained-glass windows, so the blues and the oranges and all are intersecting the clouds of incense. In the meantime, in the back of the room are these old—I can only call them, descriptively, *crones*—old, bent over, with long, black, and the black thing over them, and they are rocking back and forth to the music and clicking these coins, so as the flutes are going like this, they're clicking the coins to the sound of the flute music. The incense is surrounding everybody, and the colored light is coming through. And because it was near Christmas, in the front of the altar, there was a crèche, and in the crèche there were the

Divine figures. And these were lighting up and un-lighting up periodically with the sound of the music and the incense, and you wondered, whoa. That's how you get beyond 500. Enchantment. One becomes enchanted.

The same states arise through meditation. The same states arise through mantra. The idea is to pull back from identification with thinkingness and words and the intellect and begin to sense. So, one senses that underneath the intellect and thought is some field of awareness. Otherwise, how would you know what you're thinking or what is going on in the mind? So, this thinkingness comes to a stop, and one realizes that the stunning impact of this beauty represents the totality of the experience. I'm only breaking it down into words now, but at that time, it was the incense, the beauty, the music, the chanting, the rocking of the people to the music, the crèche with the lights flickering, and the sheer Divinity and reverence of the whole situation. So, reverence, the reverence for that which is sacred, reverence for that which is sacred, is one of the doors that opens the way to the 500s.

One now does things not out of duty, not out of fear of consequences, not out of fear of punishment by a negative, arbitrary God. One does it out of one's love for truth, out of one's devotion to lovingness as a quality and a way of life. Lovingness, as we've said, is what makes you stop and turn the beetle over on his legs. In the alley he lays there on his back, he cannot get on his own little feet, he's got a big, black—and something in you, then: compassion. So, compassion takes us beyond the 500s, compassion for all that lives.

COMPASSION FOR ALL THAT LIVES

Compassion comes up in one of the questions today, to try to complete the understanding of vegetarianism as a spiritual quality. That's this week's *Time* magazine. The cover of *Time* seems to anticipate what we're going to lecture on here all the time. Somebody's leaking info to them. Anyway, vegetarianism we have brought up before, that there are many ways of contextualizing it. It can be merely a way of sacrificing. It can be what's called *tapas*, a spiritual discipline. Not eating meat on Fridays, you see, was a way. It can be looked at various ways: as a silly superstition, or as an out-of-date, um. . . . It can be looked at many ways. It can also be seen as reverence and respect for one's religious, religious teachers. Whether it's true or not then becomes irrelevant. It's irrelevant whether eating fish on Friday is a sin or not a sin. Because the calibrated level of consciousness, the karmic consequences have to do with intention. So, we say not eating meat on a Friday is out of fear, of thinking of it as sin—because in those days, we all thought it was a sin, you'd have to confess it—is different than reverence. If you do that out of reverence, then it's a totally different motivation, huh.

So, reverence, then, for truth, and the pursuit of truth, and reverence for those who are equally committed to approaching, seeking the truth.

REVERENCE FOR LIFE

So, another way to go into the 500s is reverence. Reverence: the appreciation of that which is sacred. So, even if you don't hold it as sacred, I hold sacred that that person holds it as sacred. So, what is sacred to them I respect, because I realize that it's sacred to them even though I may not be in agreement. That allows us to appreciate difference and still respect people who think differently than we do. So, the vegetarian may do so for multiple reasons, and it would be the motivation.

Out of respect for life, it is certainly part of almost every spiritual seeker's pathway. At one time or another, the question comes up. A lot of these questions come up. Can you have sex, can you have a job, you know . . . Yoga . . . thing was renunciation, right? To renounce the world, renounce all these things.

The way of nonduality is more that one stays in the world and merely advances in one's understanding of them, moves from perception, moves out of judgmentalism, moves out of duality, and perceives them as they are. As you perceive them as they are, their beauty shines forth, so one can do it out of respect. One can do it out of reverence. One can do it out of love for the animal, reverence for its life. The Native American solved that one very well. The Great White Spirit of the Native American calibrates well over 700 and is quite a very advanced understanding of Divinity. So, the recognition of the sacredness of all life always leads to the prayer of thanking the animal and forgive him for surrendering its life. So, if you're at the level where you think that when an animal leaves its body, it dies, there would be the obstruction of thinking that you're killing, killing it. To think I can't eat it because it means killing it—"The animal doesn't really realize it just died: resist." [True.] It just goes right on in its etheric body and doesn't even pay any attention: resist." [True.] "Then comes back in another physical body and hardly notices that either: resist." [True.] "It just thinks it's one dream or another dream: resist." [True.] So, when you realize that, that nothing dies, nothing can experience death, because death is not a possibility, then it doesn't make any difference. There is a certain level, also of awareness, I've never calibrated what it is; we can do it this morning, in which you see each animal willingly surrenders its life, its physicality, to God, via you. Let me see. "That is correct: resist." [True.]

There is a point at which the animal ensures its own evolution into the oneness with Divinity. It sacrifices its physicality: "For Thee, O Lord, do I sacrifice my life. As an act of worship, I surrender my life to Thee." "That is so." [True.] I understand the animal's soul in my animal's soul, because that which I am is all that is, me and my animal soul, out of my love for God. Over and over and over again, I willingly surrender this physicality. That's my act of worship. So, as an animal, you would be depriving me, then, of one of my forms of acts of worship. That's how I express my love for God. In the presence of God, one would ask to surrender one's physicality. Anybody who's beyond 500 would become joyous at the opportunity. "If it pleases Thee, O Lord God, this physicality, I now surrender to Thee." You understand? The sacredness of the animal's soul. It's not a human soul, but all that's created by God is equally sacred. So, the animal then can only come into physicality, artificially in the numbers they do, by the fact that man breeds them. If nobody ate—I think we've said that before—if nobody ate steak, there wouldn't be any cattle out there. And who's going to raise cattle if nobody is going to eat them, you know what I mean? By their sort of being recycled through the energy fields of life, this is how they reach the completion of the potentiality of the realization of their own Divinity. The animal experiences its own Divinity. "It experiences its own Divinity without knowing its Divinity: resist." [True.] Yes. We told you that the last time too. And that's what's called "animal grace." You see the intrinsic innocence, the incredible perfection and beauty of the animal as it stands there. This happened to us, yeah, just two weeks ago. And the three or four deer stood there, and we looked at the deer, and the love just sort of like poured out, you know, by itself; their incredible stillness. You know the deer are just so fragile, they're just so slim. And the little guys are like this. And they're looking, they know that there's something in that house there. We were looking out the window at them. And they were transfixed. The deer could not move; the deer could not move. They stood there like statues. Finally, I realized that they—it was because of the energy we were pouring out, they were, like, blissed out and standing there; they weren't about to move: "That's a fact: resist." [True.] Yeah. And this one deer in particular was very sensitive to it, and I had to stop loving her and appreciating her beauty, because she couldn't move. "She was transfixed: resist." [True.] She was transfixed by the energy of adoration because of the magnificence of the beauty of Divinity within her shining forth in her grace.

* * *

Well, you see what beauty does to you, then; appreciation of beauty, it takes you right out of the intellect. I had to stop talking because the physiologic reaction of such beauty is that you start to cry; you choke up and you can't talk anymore.

So, we can adore and worship the beauty of the presence of the creator within all living things, you know, and within all form. And could I eat that deer? No, I couldn't, even at that level of consciousness. That particular deer, I couldn't, no. So that fluctuates, then, depending on where you are in your spiritual evolution. Your understanding of reality is constantly transforming. So long as you think that there's life and death, the opposite dualities of life versus death, then it would be, you might say, spiritually incorrect to kill. Once one transcends that—and I've already spoken of that too. One time in a restaurant, I suddenly realized that I *am* meat. That's what you are, man; like, forget it. So . . . I ordered a steak, and the heck with it, or something.

[Q]: "Do advanced teachers still have problems, bad habits, and neuroses?"

Well, let's finish animals first. "Can an animal ever take a human form?" "We have permission to ask this: resist." [Not true.] No. "We don't have permission to ask this: resist." Okay. We didn't ask it correctly. "This question is suitable to be asked right now: resist." [Not true.] No, not suitable. I didn't know that. "Can a human ever take an animal form? We have permission to ask that one: resist." [Not true.] No, for some reason. Once in a while, we get things that we don't know the answer why we get a *no*.

Well, we'll go back to, "Do spiritual teachers have problems, et cetera; bad habits, neuroses?" The evolution of consciousness is continuous, it's continuous. Can everybody hear me all right? It's continuous. It's more complex, actually, more complex than can really be described, because there is, first of all, the karma of being human, intrinsic to being human itself, that karma intrinsic to the physicality of humanness. The limitations of having a human brain in which the old animal brain is still functional and quite active; the whole structure of the brain down to the amygdala and the basic nuclei are reacting emotionally to massive things prior to any intellectualization. You have the collective karma. You have the collective unconscious. The thing that we created this morning had to do with something coming out of the collective unconscious. You have the karma of mankind itself. You have your own individual karma.

What appears to be a problem or bad habit or negative at one point, later on is not seen to be that way. It was only the way you were holding it. So, in other words, it isn't the reality of a thing, but your perception and your belief systems and the positionality that you have about it. If you think you cannot experience God by eating meat, then that's going to be a reality for you. As long as you keep eating meat, then you're not going to get that experience, because you're holding in your powerful mind that this is going to block you. If you think you can't experience God without going to Communion every Sunday morning, then that's going to be a limitation. So, each of these things, to say it's a problem, to say it's a limitation depends on where you are along the pathway. What's okay in a Zen monastery in Japan is not going to be okay in some other local foursquare church, let's say. So, it depends on location, which definitions, and the definitions that come automatically out of perception.

So, note the first word in this question is *problems*. Everything's a problem. Name something that isn't a problem. Everything is a problem. Is that right? Can you think of something that's not a problem? Air, there's not enough of it, it's contaminated. Space, we're running out of it. The seas are contaminated. You can't trust breathing anymore. Food's all full of poisons. All corporations are corrupt. The church is falling down. People pray, and God knows what. Everything is a problem. Having a body's a problem. Breathing in and out is a problem. Money's a problem. The future's a problem and, of course, the past is too. The past and the future are both problems, and the present is a really big problem. So, this is all how you conceptualize it. If you go back 10 years ago—go back 10 years ago now. Think ahead to this moment, from 10 years ago. This moment is not even imaginable. From 10 years ago, someone says to you, "Where will you be ten years from now on July 12," you would say, "How the hell would I know? I could be in Afghanistan." Look ahead, and you're remembering back—you're remembering back, way back—what was it, 2000 or something, the beginning of the century. We were in Arizona there one time, weren't we? You know what I mean? From the future, the present is irrelevant. From the past, the present is irrelevant. If the present is irrelevant for both the past and the future, then what relevance does it have? Any? Is it a problem? How can it be a problem if it has no relevance to anything? That takes care of the whole problem of "problem." A problem is whatever you think a problem is, you know what I'm saying.

If surrendering your life to God is something that you understand the essence of the Divinity of it, then it's a sacrament. The sacrifice of the animal is its sacrament to God, its form of expressing its value to all of life; the same with bad habits or neuroses. Anyway, but these are all perceptions. So, what is—what a person does traditionally in spiritual evolution is, they give up a thing in order to let go of their attachment in order to stop being run by it. When they become detached from it, then it doesn't make any difference whether they do it or not, because now its meaning is different. Before that, they had to let go that this is going to bring them security, this is going to bring them happiness. When you first let go of money, it's very exhilarating; you just walk around with no money on you, and everything happens fine, no problem. It's a fact. The idea that I have to have money in order to survive is an illusion. So, when you face that one, you may give up everything in the world, get an old, beat-up truck and deliver manure, you know what I mean? You still eat. And when it's lunchtime, somebody says, "You want a sandwich?" When it's breakfast time, somebody says, "Hey, you want a donut?" You go home at night and there's nothing to eat, and suddenly you find a bag of apples sitting there. Where'd they come from? I don't know. Everything just mysteriously appears of its own. Anybody who's done the *Course in Miracles* and has really tested that knows that's true. You can walk out of the house without a thing. Everything will be provided. Everything will be provided.

So, a bad habit, then, would depend on how you define it, where you are in your level of consciousness. And neuroses are really psychological problems, and all of these things come up. All of these things come up. In the evolution of consciousness, almost everyone in this audience has faced all of these things, faced all of them, with more or greater, greater or lesser success depending on the particular thing and how you're looking at it.

The impediment is almost always your belief system about it and how you're contextualizing it. How you're contextualizing it. It's your belief system about whether you eat a thing or not that is going to affect the outcome. The karmic consequence is quite different. If you see that it's irrelevant, then it doesn't really matter. Then you're either free to do it or not do it.

As far as very advanced teachers, that's a hard one to explain, because the core of that which you are is stunningly transformative and blows out everything. There is no "person" left. There is no "person" who has defects, there is no person who has neuroses, there is no person who has bad habits, so there's no reason to correct anything, because there isn't any person that you'd be correcting it about. No such deity exists.

The physicality continues on its own, and some degree of persona resumes. The jocular repartee which this persona is prone to, you know, it does it of its own. That's what persists within the world and allows for participation; otherwise, one withdraws. So, for some years, there's nothing going on in the world of any sufficient interest to get you reinvolved in it. You don't read the newspaper for 10 years, 20 years. You don't bother watching television. You don't go anywhere. You don't hear anything. There's nothing to read or there's nothing to know, so there's no pursuit of knowledge, you see. And because of the passing illusion of perception, there's a loss of interest in the world and its events. And if President Reagan got shot or something, you don't find it out until a couple months later. Somebody mentions it; you say, "You're kidding. You're kidding." You missed it altogether, because it wasn't of that sufficient—you weren't focused on the world.

Most of the time, when the person reaches a very advanced level of consciousness, they cease and desist from human life and affairs. The majority of people who reach very advanced levels of consciousness are never heard from again. Only with great rarity and after considerable effort is there the return of the capacity to function in the world, much less to master both simultaneously. So, what you say would be a problem would be a way in which something is being looked at. Other people see problems in situations where I don't see any problems. As far as I'm concerned, that's just the way it is. And, uh, say people kill each other and millions die. You say, "Yeah, that's right, that's right." "Well, shouldn't you be out there parading for peace?" You say: "Oh, I think somebody should, but not me." Ten million come, ten million go; they're going to keep cycling back and forth—ten million more of them, century after century. This goes on, and so you see the flow of the nature of life, and there's no desire to try to enter the river and change its course, huh, because the wisdom of God prevails.

Nothing escapes, what do we say, the karmic unity of the unmanifest to manifest, and what it manifests is one karmic totality in absolutely perfectly balanced unity. And there's really no necessity to do anything about it whatsoever, because it evolves of its own nature, because the progression of consciousness is innate within the nature of consciousness itself, and it doesn't need your help!

That's a thing as a teacher you have to—that's another whole block about teaching or not teaching, and the meaning and the significance and the value. And then, of course, there's nobody left to teach, so it either happens or it doesn't happen, and it has to do with the karmic coherence of—at a certain point, one transcends personal karma. But one does not transcend the karmic intention of Divinity, does not escape the karmic consequence. That's why the Luciferic mistake of selling out integrity for power over others, when you see that there's no negative God that you're going to have to be answerable to, is an error. At the level at which that temptation comes in, it's very strong and very cleverly and convincingly phrased. And many are the gurus who have fallen for it: fame and fortune and power over others. See, because the lie which is Luciferically expressed is correct within content, but it ignores the context—that you have not escaped the destiny of God, hm? You may have escaped your own personal karmic destiny. At a certain level beyond 600, you are not really answerable for it in a personal way, but one is still within the karmic coherence of the totality of the context of God. So, you are not beyond karma; you are only beyond personal karma. But boy, you're sure within the powerful karmic field of the infinite presence of Almighty God. And that is the sad discovery once the mistake is made. You just sacrificed all for illusion.

GOD IS THE INFINITE CONTEXT

God being the infinite context, then, is the ultimate infinite possibility of all that exists, all of which is kept within a karmic perfect balance. That's why you don't have to fear judgment, because everything comes about as a result of the essence of its own expressing itself within the context of God. It's inescapable. There's no such thing as a murderer getting away with it. People say, "Oh, he got away with it." Yeah, right, he got away with it. Big joke of the century. Nobody gets away with *anything*, because *all* is noticed, and that's what kinesiology is based on. Kinesiology is based on inherent coherence, which is guaranteed by its essence as Divinity, that nothing escapes the infinite Allness of God and is registered forever within an accessible field that we call "Consciousness." So, that is the whole basis of the test of kinesiology: that that which *is* registers within consciousness forever, all that ever is or has been, and therefore, all truth stands revealed. All truth is accessible. Anything that has ever happened is accessible.

Our own search for spiritual truth, then, tends to influence our family for better or worse. They may even think you're crazy and decide they're going to go in the opposite direction. I've seen people who're not too evolved look directly at an incredible miracle witnessed by all kinds of people and not even see it; much less do they understand the miraculous nature of what they just witnessed. In fact, they go into denial of what they just saw. It's very interesting, the incapacity to see the obvious—so, people live in different realities. So, what—because of one's level of consciousness, then, what would be a problem, a bad habit, or a neurosis would depend on what level you're at. Any more questions about that? Because people do worry about such things. Hmm.

When you reenergize the persona in order to react to the ways of the world—the persona is a habitual set of knowing social behaviors and the remnant of one's former identity, which is retained sort of in the memory of the persona. It isn't what you are, but it was the accumulation of the collected images of the world in yourself about that which you are. And it's sort of like an astral shell, goes on its own trajectory. One gives it, you might say, sufficient energy to enable the continuance of a human lifetime, especially if you reenter the world to continue it, but that's arbitrary. One can disconnect at any time! One can get involved with the movie to the degree that everybody else that's in the movie thinks you're in the movie with them, and everybody's happy. The only difference is, you can walk out of it in an instant. It's just a matter of will. But when you walk out of it, it's not always that easy to come back. It takes effort to reenergize, to reenergize that which the world would call a relatively normal lifetime. The lifetime is never really normal again, anyway, not really, no; but it does conform to human society sufficiently to return to a functioning. This has also its karmic commitments that may bring it about.

We see what happened to some people. We see that Ramana Maharshi, for instance, suddenly fell down as a teenager and thought he was dying, and, uh, was pretty much left for dead, I think. The bugs were eating him up, and he was dehydrated and stopped eating, and so it takes time. He was silent and didn't speak for two years. So, it takes time to reenergize, and it's usually—it's always because of the input of people around you to eat and breathe and sleep and do all those things. And the love of such people then begins to get the bug to stir again like it's coming out of its winter hibernation. So, the hibernated remains of what the potentiality is for a human can then be revived through the energy input.

The effect on a family of our own spiritual effort, then, is both good and bad. On the one hand, it may energize them. We certainly can set examples at certain levels that we can implement. I think crossing over 200 is something where the spiritual seeker in the family does have an impact. To insist on integrity, to insist on the demonstration of integrity is one where external pressure does have an effect. And that is—at a place where I'm chief of staff, the rehabilitation of these children has to do with trying to get them to the level of integrity, to admit that "I am responsible for my own action." Because you can't get above integrity until you say, "Yes, I'm the one that did that." So long as you're blaming Gimbels for falling on the ice on the sidewalk, you're still below 200, because Gimbels didn't push you over on the ice front; it was how you put your feet. You saw it was icy. You're 52 years old, and if you don't know how to put your feet on ice, you shouldn't be walking on the ice in front of Gimbels, much less suing them, so I've never had much sympathy for putting the blame "out there," because of the loss of spiritual integrity. *I'm* the one that was careless about where I put my feet, and if it—see what I mean? Every ding in the car, I take responsibility for. I mean, it was my thoughtlessness that allowed for it. So, that kind of training we can teach our children. I think we can inspire them to become integrous and to feel the increase of power and energy that goes with integrity. And if you teach them by example and keep bringing to their awareness that there is a certain payoff in self-esteem which nobody sees. Yes, you don't have to pick it up, you don't have to pick it up, you don't have to pick it up, but when you do, over and over again, suddenly you notice a difference in how you feel about yourself, and that's called "self-esteem."

So, I think that the building of self-esteem through integrity is something we can certainly do. People remember EST [Erhard Seminars Training] from back in the '60s or '70s; I forget when EST was... the '70s. Yeah, well, what Werner Erhard was trying to teach—I mean, he had his own problems, but aside from that, what he was trying to do was get everybody over 200. He wanted everybody to be over integrity, take responsibility that you're creating your own experience. And of course, everybody went through shock, they took away your watch and your lipstick and, *ha!* You couldn't go to the bathroom, you couldn't eat, you couldn't drink water, no tea, no coffee. It was a real big shock, and people went through all kinds of agonies. And it's really, you know, it brought up a lot of compassion, you'd see people lying there crying and desperate because she couldn't have her lipstick or she couldn't have her watch, or they had to go to the bathroom. I mean, all these trivial childhood things, and they were going through these horrible agonies, almost, you know, going through major crises, major crises, major nervous breakdowns over some little habit. It's lunchtime and they're not having their lunch: crisis. So, it was a very interesting experience, and I thought that anybody who loved their kids would send them to EST, you know, because EST could do what you couldn't do as a parent, you know. It was very intense training, but you also learned very rapidly. And after that, you never worried about making it to the bathroom ever again. If you just resist it and resist, it disappears! Now you don't have to go to the bathroom at all. Ah! That's quite a discovery, to go through the crisis of the bladder and come out victorious. You had to go, you had to go, and you don't know when you're going to go, and you don't go, and then all of a sudden, it disappears. You're rid of that habit; it disappears. If you withstand it and transcend it, a couple minutes beyond that, you don't have to go anymore. We can stop now, we don't have to go anymore. So, you just crossed another barrier. So, I think those are things that we can really encourage our children . . . is integrity.

* * *

So, the main emphasis was how to transcend the 400s, how to get to the 500s. As we know, only 0.4 percent of the population, 4 percent of the population ever gets to 500; 4 percent of the population transcends 500; and 0.4 gets to 540, 540 is unconditional love. So, those are, those are the ways out of the box: through love, joy, peace, beauty, consideration, devotion, respect for others, the love we have for our animals whether we eat them or not, to see the Divinity of the presence of their love. As we said, the dog's wagging tail calibrates at 500, and a kitty's purr calibrates at 500. So, that which we respect in the animal, then, is not its animal-ness, but its love. We always—it's the lovingness of the animal that we respect. And it's why people go to such extremes for the animal. We say, "Well, they're really a nut about an animal." No, it's about the love; that's the love that's present. We had a staff meeting, and this girl who was very, very nasty and very, very mean, and had a long, mean, nasty—"I'll stab you to death," and using all kinds of four-letter words, and she's sitting there at the staffing, just defiantly hostile and just as soon kill you as look at you, and then her parents came in from the reservation. Her parents came in and walked in the door. They'd traveled five hours to reach her. Instantly you could feel the love light up the room. All that stuff disappeared. All the irrelevance of all what had been. And the reality was the love. You could see the love of the girl, her joy and their joy eclipsed everything else, and you're over 500. Reason . . . at the level of 400, they should put her away already and keep her there; she's not safe on the street. But when you saw the capacity for love, the capacity to respond to love, and the value that both sides held for the love, then you knew that it was all going to end up all right. So, that is the main way out, then: love, joy, peace, enlightenment, the appreciation for beauty, the respect for beauty; and I think that's the way to the 500s.

* * *

I'll have to tell you the truth about slavery. It's a great advance in human consciousness. Slavery's a great advance in human consciousness. Does that make sense? No? Well, I just want you to understand how positionality, positionality creates right and wrong, truth, untruth, et cetera.

You see, in the olden days, when the great hordes swept across Europe, the Vandals and the Visigoths, and the Mongols and the Huns, and all these people. In the good old days when the hordes would sweep into civilization, the Roman Empire was a very tempting plum. But one horde after another would sweep down and try to knock out the Roman Empire. And of course, they just killed all the—they just killed the people. And the hordes did the same thing; they just killed people. When you conquered somebody, you took their gold, you had sex with the women, and you killed everybody. Then one day, a smart guy says, "Hey, these people are worth something." *Ha!* Decided, "We won't kill 'em. Hey, let's save 'em." And they began to sell them. Wow, they're valuable! Human beings became valuable. We won't just massacre and kill them. The Japanese in Nanjing massacred what, 30,000, or 300,000. If they were more evolved, they would have captured them as slaves and sold them, right? They weren't that far advanced.

So, all of a sudden, the value of the life of a human being dawned on people: they're worth money. Well, that's somewhere up the line, isn't it? I mean, you're moving in the right direction, folks. Anyway, he moved up to—we got up to greed, anyway. He was worth something on the market. So much a pound, you know; they used to put the slave up there and feel him, and if he had muscles like me, they'd put him in the bargain basement. People now had a value. Slavery was an advance in human consciousness from just slaughtering everybody out of hatred and seeing them as worthless and potential garbage. So, slavery, from that point of view was an advance. It would be better to be captured, and even a few hundred years ago, this meant your lifespan was twice as long because you were valued as a worker. One got medical care, food, housing, clothing. So, you see how it depends on how you look at slavery. From that viewpoint, it was the beginning of the realization of the worth of human life and the value of preserving it.

So, anything in history depends on how you contextualize it and how you perceive it, and the positionality you take about it. And if you're perfecting moving up from Apathy to Greed—you see, to become greedy is a big move out of Sloth, huh? You know, that's the effect television had on the great unwashed. They began to see what's possible, and up comes, "I want that." Up comes anger. Anger's got a lot of energy; 150 can get you off your butt. Down here, they just lay around in the gutter, drinking gin and letting the babies die of starvation, you know?

Anyway, the pirate was into greed, into greed, you see. And making money was more valuable than human life. So, he had a lot to learn, painfully as it was.

* * *

There's a couple of things I just want to be sure to mention before I get taken away by these questions. Oh, let's see. We wanted to mention that slavery was an advance in civilization, which most people wouldn't think about. There was a lady who became famous. There was a movie made *about* her and a bestseller, and all about her lion and her life with her lion, and uh, *Born Free* or something, and we asked people if they knew what happened to her in the end. What was the end of the story, years after the movie and the book? The lion killed her, yeah. The lion ate her up. So, people said, "Isn't that awful, after all that love and devotion, books, movies, and everything, lots of . . . her love for this lion? He turned on her and killed her." Then I heard the story. I know what the lion did. The lion adored her; he loved her so much, he just ate her up. He just ate her up because he loved her so much. He just—and you know, in language, we still say, you know, "You're so pretty, I could eat you up." You want to eat up that which you love. So, the lion did not eat—kill her out of hatred or any kind of evil; he killed her out of love. "The lion ate her up because he adored her: resist." [True.] Correct. He ate her out of love. So, you see, when you're already in a very high space of love yourself, you see it where other people don't see it. You see the love of the animal that sacrifices itself to the glory of God by serving man, and you see that the lion kills the lady because he adored her. So, what you see, then, is really representing your capacity. At a certain level, you see love in all, all things.

WATCH OUT FOR THE WOLF IN SHEEP'S CLOTHING

We wanted to talk about the lady that got eaten out of love; how slavery's an advance, oh yes. I was looking at the naivete of mankind, you know, the naivete, and realizing that there's another level of integrity which you never hear mentioned. And that is to take responsibility for your own naivete, and to become the shepherd of your own sheep. So, Jesus said, you know, "Watch out for the wolf in sheep's clothing," but the wolf in sheep's clothing eats people all the time. Having been warned of that, then, how does one protect oneself? Well, until we discovered that kinesiology discerns truth from falsehood, there was no objective means of doing it, and therefore it was said, "By their fruits ye shall know them." And that which radiates beauty, grace, love, and peace, you can tell is of God. And that which radiates its opposite is not of God. Because consciousness is like the hardware of a computer, it doesn't know right from wrong, doesn't know truth from falsehood; every great sage that's ever lived has said that man is innocent on a certain level due to ignorance. Because the hardware, software could tell the difference, but you're born only with the hardware. You're born with hardware.

Consciousness is like the hardware, and the programs are what society programs you with. Because your own hardware can't tell truth from falsehood, it cannot discern and has no control over what it's being programmed by. People get programmed as they walk by an advertisement coming off their television. They don't know that they just got programmed, but I can pick it up later with hypnosis and with kinesiology that he just got programmed. The message is already imprinted. He didn't have any say over it. He didn't say, "Gee, do I want to believe this? Do I want this imprinted on my consciousness?" You don't have any, like, selection over what goes into your software. The older you get, the more sophisticated you get; you get some selection of what you—you can pick what movies you want to see. And the movies that glamorize that which is nonintegrous, you learn to avoid it, because you realize your own susceptibility and vulnerability to the glamorization of it. There's a movie out now, I haven't calibrated it, but it glamorizes Chicago gangsters in the '30s or something, which has its glamour.

BECOME THE SHEPHERD OF YOUR OWN SHEEP

To "become the shepherd of your own sheep," then, means to acknowledge that all the subpersonalities within you, the child in you, the adolescent, all those things that still are there, are now your responsibility, and because you're awake now, because you're awake—more awake than the rest of them within you—you have to become the shepherd that guards the innocence of the sheep within you. Yeah. You take responsibility. You take responsibility now and say, "I recognize that my mind can't tell truth from falsehood. As a consequence . . . as a consequence, I will not put myself in a position where that naivete can lead to deleterious results." You know what I'm saying? It's like not throwing your pearls before swine. I never cared for the language of that, but you have to take responsibility now for what you allow yourself to be programmed by. The glamorization of every kind of negativity by the current media is probably the *biggest* source of negativity, the biggest input into the consciousness of mankind right now. I would say if it were not for the media right now, the consciousness of mankind would probably be 10 points higher than it is.

And the blatant, the blatant nonintegrity of video games and things like that which are shocking—they're so shocking that even the media that put out negativity around the clock were shocked by it. Just two weeks ago, there was a new one out in which the graphics of it even shocked people that can't be shocked anymore. It's training children how to kill women, you know, how to attack them and kill them, et cetera. And here's this mother—this came to my mind as I watched this mother on TV; she says, "Well, I don't see anything wrong with that. He knows it's just a game." No. The unconscious *doesn't* know it's a game. That's the whole point. He does *not* know that it's just a game. This is becoming a programmed, trained killer. When he shoots his classmates: "I just did it to see what it felt like." Hmm. Just for kicks. "Did you hate those people?" "No." Whoa! I mean, that is really serious. If you kill the people you hate, it at least makes sense. Now you're beyond any kind of logic, reason, sensibility; any restraint, any restraint at all. So, now people are being programmed into nonintegrity via nonlinear programming. That is probably the worst downside I've ever seen in human history. Why? Because you don't have a choice.

So, we have to own that the innocence is our vulnerability, is our vulnerability. And I think it's the answer of certain energies to the advancing spiritual awareness of the populace. The answer of that which would rather maintain its control—because it did, at the level of 190, until the late '80s—had control of this planet. It feels control slipping, and now it's found a way to program the minds of young children as they are sitting there, until they're hopelessly in their camp. And they don't even know they are in their camp. You just got brainwashed, and you don't even know you've been brainwashed. That's a hard one to break out of, huh? And it's the most serious condition, I think, on the planet right now. But when you're buying your kid a nice game for his birthday party and train his little mind to become expert at evil, and then the mother sits there on TV, "Well, he knows it's just a game," I thought, "Oh God, mother." This must be the worst mother on the planet. I hate her this instant, you know what I mean? She's just sold her son down the drain, you know? She thinks it's just a harmless amusement, it's just a game. So, we said to take responsibility, to be the shepherd of your own sheep. And that is the awareness that within yourself, within the various archetypes, the subpersonalities, is still the programmable; the programmable. And to watch what you're being, to be aware. All right?

* * *

So, now we were going to talk about that, and we talked about that from the past, if we go back 20 years from now, this moment would be irrelevant, you know, not even conceivable and certainly unimportant, not worth a nickel. Twenty years from now, you won't even remember it, you know what I mean. I remember I went to a lecture by somebody or other one time, and you know, it was exciting and fun, and I don't remember it, really. Twenty years from now, it will only be part of the, part of the mosaic of your own lifetime, you see. So, we said that in reality, in the space of the Presence, there is either "then," "now," or in the "future." That the focus on "now"—that "now" itself is equally an illusion as the past and the future. This is more advanced and sophisticated, but if there's no "then," neither is there any reality called "now." Hmm. Outside of time is neither "then," nor the "future"; nor is there a "now." Well, if there's no past and there's no future, and there's no "now," then where are you? Where are we? I don't know. Outside of time someplace. I just ask the question.

So, there's questions here having to do with the karma of various ethnic groups, and all. You see, we've only been sort of investigating a new way of understanding and gaining knowledge about spirituality. It hasn't been around that long, and any one of these aspects in itself could take a lifetime. You can take any one little aspect of this chart, because these calibrated levels are very gross, these are very gross, you know, because there's a great many variations of all these things. There's anxiety, there's terror, there's nervousness. I mean, there's all kinds of fear, right? There's desiringness, cravingness, wantingness, having to have this, just wantingness; so, there's subtleties and gradations of all these. There's quite a bit of difference between 100 and 101, because that's a logarithm. That's quite a bit of difference.

So, I could spend a lifetime as a young man now researching just this field here, just this field here; how it arose, how it expresses itself, all the subtle variations; calibrate everything from 100 to 105. It'd take you a lifetime. Every variation: 100.1, 100.12, 100.13, because already, because it's logarithmic, there's quite a difference, there's quite a difference. So, even a 10th of one percent. So, in a way, we're saying we not only got this telescope; we can look up into the heavens and we see these galaxies and we see the moons around Mars, or whatever it is Galileo ran into—but that was only the beginning of many, many lifetimes. How many astronomers, over how many decades, are still just barely breaking through the surface of the subject? So, we're at a rudimentary state, you know, but just to contextualize the evolution of human consciousness in this way, in itself, already has a transformative effect. Thank you, Lord. What'd I say? I'll say it backward.

* * *

Now, let's see. Now we're going to go through these questions. I'm going to repeat the questions so we can hear them. That's the value of having them written, is that we can repeat them.

[Q]: "There's a lot said about meditation and reason as pathways to the presence of God. What of athletic endeavor?"

So, we said that what sets the karmic consequence, what sets the calibrated level is intention, intention. And I think I did mention that, yes, in *Power vs. Force*, because the intention of the athlete not only has quite an effect on his performance, but certainly has a profound karmic consequence. One can do anything in the name of the love of God and to be of service to God. And peeling potatoes for your family is to me as holy as praying up a storm in church. Everybody runs to church and prays up a storm. But the test of the oatmeal is at the kitchen sink. That's where the test is. Anybody can feel holy at church with the hymns going, everybody feels holy. Everybody feels holy at church. That doesn't do you much good. If you can see the devotion, the sacrificing of oneself for the love of others, then peeling every potato is as holy as any other act, and therefore, athletics, because athletics can demonstrate your joy at your existence, your thankfulness to God for this body and the joy of it at the present time, and it's a way of demonstrating one's love and devotion to God.

At a certain point of endeavor, physical endeavor, athletics being probably the most common one, you of course run against the ultimate barrier. One of those books I read about it, I don't know which one. Anyway, there is a barrier beyond which you cannot go. You cannot run one iota faster, you cannot lift one more ounce, you cannot lift one more box in the warehouse, you cannot lift one more rock, you cannot put one more arm over your head, you cannot take another stroke in the water; you've reached *it*, the limit, the barrier, the blockade. At that point, with grim, absolute determination, one can by intention and will—you then discover how powerful the will is. The will is the crux of finding God. You *will* yourself through that barrier, *absolutely*, at any price, and crash! You go through the barrier. The next rock doesn't weigh anything. You lift it effortlessly. And I've lifted rocks for 12, 15, 18 hours, 150-pound rocks, nonstop; didn't even feel tired. I had to turn the headlights to the car on, because the whole work crew had long left, and they'd all fallen over.

So, this is the most common place that this is experienced, I think, is in sports. Everybody knows that the four-minute-mile barrier, Roger Bannister—and once he broke it, then many others broke it. So, athletics is another way of breaking that barrier of the sense of "I can't" and the realization that there is no limit, really, and one can break through it. Yes, I did describe, I discovered that in a work situation. I couldn't lift one more box, and willing myself through that barrier, suddenly all the boxes became lightweight. I was just amazed. I could hardly lift those crazy boxes of canned peas in a pea cannery, 110 degrees and no windows in this warehouse, and you couldn't lift one more box. And that was when there was that discovery. And people who jog discover that: a certain barrier, and all of a sudden, your jogging is effortless, and you're in a state of high joy. And the jogging is doing itself. You're not doing the jogging; the jogging is jogging itself because it's effortless. And I think that's where the Sufi dancers discover it too, where they—And I also discovered it at dancing. There's a certain point in which you stop dancing, and you are being danced; just like the boxes were being lifted and the rocks were being lifted, and the runner finds it is effortless.

In spiritual, serious spiritual work, if a person's really committed to enlightenment, you're going to run up against that barrier more than once. There's that barrier beyond which you cannot go, and yet you have to go beyond it, and you summon up all the spiritual power and intention you have, and by the intention of will and fixity of will, you break through the barrier and the impossible becomes possible. That also happens at around 600, calibrated level 600; somebody asked me about that. There's that beyond which you cannot go, and you go beyond it, and bam, you're in a new universe; you're in a new dimension of reality, a new dimension of reality.

The thinkingness—there's a point beyond which thinkingness will not get you any further, and there's an absolute surrender of, absolute surrender of the thinkingness. And suddenly, the knowingness stands there where the thinkingness was blocking it before. The knowingness stands there.

That's overcoming that block, and in spiritual work, everybody knows there is that block where you cannot go further. I think saying the rosary or spinning the prayer wheel are all efforts to transcend that limit. "I cannot say the rosary one more time." "I cannot say the Jesus Prayer one more time." Who is that famous—I don't think he was a Jesuit; I think he was a monk who just repeated the Jesus Prayer, period. That's all he did. There's this famous little book about him. And when you couldn't do it one more time, he did it one more time and broke through.

[Q]: "What do you do when, in spite of all the spiritual work and surrender, you still feel trapped and it seems at a dead end?"

I already answered that, didn't I? Huh, it's only when you feel you're at a dead end that you make a major breakthrough. As long as you think things are going swimmingly, they may or may not be.

[Q]: "What about the American Indian? Because of their level of consciousness, how is it that they suffered such fate at the hands of the Europeans?"

You'd have to check out the karma of the American Indian and see who they were, and what they brought about upon themself. Besides, what happened to them culturally, again is from the viewpoint of illusion. We'd say, "Well, it was a disaster." It was sociologically; it was from a prosaic level of reason. Each of these things, to get the real answer, you have to go beyond the apparent and go beyond what common logic or reason would make you think or see and find out whether or not it was liberation. How do you know when a thing is catastrophe or liberation? Because it was out of catastrophe that liberation arose in this one here. It was at the depths of hell. You'd say, "Well, the depths of hell after all that spiritual seeking, how can that be fair?" Yeah. Well, it smashed the last finger to let go, heh heh. It's that old joke—you know, a guy hanging over the edge of the cliff with one finger, and God says, "Let go." And the guy says, looking up, "Is there anybody else up there?"

[Q]: "After the experience of God, is one's level of consciousness raised over 400, et cetera?"

Well, everyone's experience of God does have, of course, a profound effect, and a near-death experience is transformative. A near-death experience calibrates, um . . . people calibrate considerably higher after it. Out-of-body experience, there's generally no major shift of consciousness. However, there is a shift of awareness. There's the awareness that you're not a physical body. When you're out there in the middle of space, it's sort of space in the middle of space, and the body's laying there in the bed. It's rather clear that you're not that, because you're out here and it's there. It always amazed me that consciousness didn't go up from an out-of-body experience. "Consciousness advances due to out-of-body experience: resist" [Not true.] Isn't that funny? "This lifetime, out of that bed, consciousness advanced itself: resist." [Not true.] It didn't, no. Because I was visible when I came back in the body. Anyway, it certainly was startling, I'll tell you; it was just like flying without wings. You say, "Whoa," I mean . . . that was amazing, though, that out-of-body experience, because you *are* aware that you're the etheric body, you're not the physical body. It seems to me like that would raise your consciousness level, so I don't know the reason for that. Maybe it's because, um—oh, that's the expression and not the cause. Oh, I see; I'm seeing it as cause.

"So, the going out of body is already the realization of the truth that you're not a physical body: resist." [True.] Oh, okay, it now makes sense. The reason you go out of body is, you're already aware on a certain level that you're not a physical body, and that sort of allows for the experience in the first place. I was looking at it the other way around, uh huh.

Transcending the Intellect through Beauty | 47

[Q]: "Did the consciousness level of mankind raise after 9/11?"

I think we asked that before, and it said no. It is advancing. I expect it to accelerate. Why? Because the power of even one person over, you know, 500 is so enormous that you get a few individuals on the planet that are in the high 500s, they're going to already raise, and a few in the 600s or 700s. Mankind is just going to keep going like that, and the more that go up, the more that is going to cross the line, and the more that cross the line, I expect to see mankind get pulled right up into higher and higher levels of consciousness.

At the time of Jesus Christ, the consciousness level of mankind was 100. 100. It took it 2,000 years to go from 100 to 190, and then in the late '80s, then in the late '80s, it went to 207. Now it's up to 208; now it's up to 209. So now it's moving very rapidly, very rapidly. You see, I think the decimation of the corporate world, and 9/11, and all those things, the net effect is that integrity becomes more important.

[Q]: "How can the consciousness of the world mind be raised to 500, and can it ever be done?"

It isn't like it's "done"; it's like it evolves. My feeling about the advancement of human consciousness over the millennia is that consciousness—when we go back to the age of the reptiles, we go back to the age of the dinosaurs, we see that the energy field of life on earth was 70. If we go 500 millions before that, we keep going to lower numbers. So, we see that life emerges, that consciousness—it's within the essence of consciousness to constantly evolve, to constantly evolve. So, we would expect then that there would be a time in the future when the consciousness level of mankind would be up to 500, huh? Shall we all vote for that? I'm in favor. Okay.

* * *

I'm interested in the overall level of consciousness of mankind itself. How it expresses itself in individuals is relatively immaterial. It's the totality of it that spells the quality of life on this planet. Um, there are, of course, whole continents where the level of consciousness is very near the bottom, and it seems to be the karmic pattern. It's as though one comes in from a very low level of consciousness and is born into a very low level of consciousness which is just a little higher than where they were, maybe. And then there's a recycling in coming back into higher and higher levels of consciousness. Consciousness seems to evolve, evolve over great expanses of time. And my suspicion is that that's because that's its essence, just as an oak tree grows. Within the acorn is already that karmic propensity.

Any experience, I think any spiritual experience tends to raise one's level of consciousness—certainly, the near-death experience; we can calibrate that. Any sense of closeness and oneness with God increases the sensitivity to beauty and appreciation for the value of all of life and increases the consciousness level of all of mankind. The effect of more advanced levels of consciousness on the totality of human consciousness is to raise it. And we did the mathematics on that one time, and I forget the numbers, but each person at 500 is offsetting the negative effect of probably tens of thousands of people at the lower level. Were it not so, mankind would drown in its own negativity and self-destruct. So, each forgiveness, each decision to love instead of hate, every move we make in a spiritual direction helps bring all of mankind up to the ultimate level, which we certainly hope would be 500.

[Q]: *"How does the body respond to a negative or positive statement independent of the mind?"*

Well, that's asking about the kinesiologic test itself. The kinesiologic test is impersonal. It's a response of life in its expression as protoplasm, to the presence of truth or falsehood—you know, the presence of truth or the absence of truth, to be very strict. So, it's almost like analogous to protoplasm. Consciousness recognizes truth, and like an electrostatic condenser, it recognizes electrons, but it does not recognize protons or positrons. So, consciousness then is beyond personal belief, so it's beyond mind in that it's not within your capacity to change it. Any of the questions that we ask, everybody will get the same answer to, irrespective of what your belief system is about it. That's a quality of consciousness itself, that it recognizes the reality of truth. Anybody who's done the *Course in Miracles* recognizes that statement, that only the real is real, and therefore, the reason there's nothing to fear is because only the real is real. The unreal simply does not exist. That's what the kinesiologic test confirms, is that which is integrous makes you go strong; that which is not integrous, because it has no reality, you go weak because the electric is off, you might say. In the presence of truth, the electric goes on and you go strong. In the absence of truth, you don't have a negative; you just have the absence of truth, and because there's an absence of truth, there's no electricity running down the wire and you have no strength. So, you drop—you're dropping because of the absence of the truth and not because of the presence of negativity.

[Q]: "Is there evolution in society amongst its leaders in the material, practical world of business, education, and politics?"

And I do believe that these are going to become demanded. I do believe that if nothing else, we can count on good, old greed to make sure we become integrous. If you own stock in the company, you want to make sure the guy you put in as president calibrates over 200. You know what I mean? It's on every page. You can see that nonintegrity takes you down the tubes. It takes you to bankruptcy, it takes you to bankruptcy. Also, of course, the higher the level of spiritual awareness, consciousness, the people are healthier. We know that raising people's level of consciousness—the *Course in Miracles* is everybody's common experience of that—is that the higher the level of consciousness, the greater the degree of health, the greater the resistance to disease. I've come to believe, or come to observe, let's say, that all illnesses are cyclic. So, every patient I see in the office—I hardly see any patients at all anymore; I've given up practically all the practice, but occasionally I still have some patients. And when I see a patient, the one thing I tell them is that *all* illnesses are cyclic. Every single illness that exists is cyclic. What does that mean? It means it comes and it goes. It tends to come and go. By its nature, that which wasn't there and now has come, it must in this essence be temporary, because therefore, if it was a reality, it wouldn't have come; it would have always been. So, if it's a temporariness that had an onset, then it has to have also an exit ramp. That which came in on an entrance ramp has to have an exit ramp, exit ramp as well. Consequently, all illnesses cycle in and out. What helps them to cycle out is advance—first of all, wearing out the karmic propensity in the first place; secondly, the negative belief systems that are supporting it, and I think they karmically cycle out. So, I tell everybody, every illness I've ever seen comes and goes. Every one has the capacity to go. If it hasn't gone yet with you, then there's more you got to be doing about it, or you just simply have to be willing to wear out the karmic timing of it.

Let's see, I lived a pretty bad life as a pirate, there, for a number of years, you know. And put a lot of people over the side and killed a lot of infidels and stuff. So, I don't know. How much suffering and how many whatchamacallits do you have to put in for that? I don't know. I went through the surgery there without anesthesia, and it was excruciating. In the middle of it, I remembered exactly what I did to that guy with a spear; and I remember it *exactly*. So, how much pain and physical suffering would satisfy my unconscious that I had now paid that off? Do you have to satisfy God with your suffering? No. What would God want with your suffering? I mean, suffering is a penny-ante game. Why would the infinite God of all creation be interested in whether you suffer or not? He'd be bored to tears. Wouldn't it—"More suffering, oh give me a break," huh. "Hey, that's the old suffering ploy: 'Oh God, look how I suffer.'" Oh wow. So, we have to get off that suffering is holy, stop genuflecting and dropping to our knees and worshipping suffering and pain. The God that we are speaking of is not pleased with suffering and pain. Is not pleased. "We ask permission to ask that: resist." [True.] "That's a fact: resist." [True.] No, God doesn't get off on your pain and suffering. So, who's getting off on your pain and suffering? The judge: the savage, cruel, sadistic, unrelenting, unmerciful inner judge. And it's in each one of us. Never underrate the judge. There's no degree of cruelty this judge won't go to, hmm. No amount of suffering. Twenty years of agony, hey, those are just jacks for openers. Talk to me in another 20.

So, this savage, unrelenting . . . ah, you see, unconsciously the person is afraid of losing their soul to hell. Out of fear of the damnation of your soul to hell for sin, you will put yourself through unbelievable, exquisite agony. "That's the truth: resist." [True.] By God, it's the truth. I know, because I lived it and agonized over it and discovered it in my own unconscious and had to undo it, and it took a lot of spiritual work, because that's deeply rooted and confounded by certain interpretations of religion, that suffering is good for the soul. And, um, okay.

So, the enemy is not some external god who gets off on exterminating people in the most painful way possible, but it's in yourself. So, I recently discovered that configuration in that collective, that only by pain, and suffering and pain, can you save your soul. So, this looks to pain and suffering as the savior. It's the reverse of Christianity, in a way. Your savior is pain and suffering because the more pain and suffering, the more God's wrath will be assuaged. And your pain and suffering is therefore saving your soul. I asked, why would anybody put themselves through years and years of so much intense agony? It just makes no sense. The dread and fear of one's soul being thrown into eternal damnation is a terror, and that is the grip that the old Freudian superego has on you. And there's a whole archetype in the unconscious that energizes that. So, prayer and meditation on that, the willingness to forgive oneself, and the undoingness of that; the willingness to be merciful toward yourself and toward anyone and everyone.

In psychoanalysis, we all—you know, I did psychoanalysis, and I had a classical psychoanalysis, very successful; very brilliant analyst and very successful analysis. In psychoanalytic training, you're trained to always approach the patient from the side of the superego. Before you start pulling up what's in the unconscious, you first ameliorate the superego, which is the conscience. Otherwise, the patient's going to be attacked by—so, if you bring up incestuous wishes while you still have a fierce and malignant superego, the person's going to go into a suicidal depression, you know what I'm saying? So, with the patient's positive transference, you begin to ameliorate their savage superego. "How could I have done that to"—they want to die on the floor, because they made a faux pas in society. So, you start working on this savage superego. You don't want to expose them to the executioner, because until you start pulling up what's in the id, making a faux pas in society is very minimal; you know, the death wishes you have toward people, the teachers you wish would die, and stuff. Wait until all that stuff comes up. So, you have to ameliorate the severity of your own conscience and see that it's irrational. It's not God. Everybody thinks that their savage superego and a big, massive sense of guilt means they're holy. No, it means you're neurotic. You need a good analyst.

I had some forbidden thought. I remember I was laying on the couch, and I was shaking. This terror came up, you know. And I . . . he says, "Now what?" I said, "I can't talk." He said, "What is it?" I said, "It's terror." Terror. And the terror was a forbidden thought coming up. A forbidden thought coming up. So, I projected onto my analyst, you know, this savage killer. And I'll never forget the time I broke through my classic obsessive-compulsive, phobic anxiety disorder for which I was seeing him every day, plus being a training analyst five days a week, all the way from New York City into his office on East 88th and 3rd Street. And the terror got bigger and bigger and bigger. Oh my God! You know, people nowadays . . . it's stylish to put down Freud. You should lay on the couch every day for a couple of months and see how much you put down Freud. Anyway, I'm laying on the couch, and all of a sudden, all this stuff comes out of nowhere, and he hasn't said anything or done anything to bring it up. I started getting phobic. I couldn't go through a tunnel, I couldn't go over a bridge. I had claustrophobia, I couldn't get on an elevator; I couldn't be in crowds, and I couldn't be by myself. I couldn't go under the river or over the river. His name was Dr. Ovesey. So, I said, "Good God, I'm getting worse. This analysis is making me worse." He said, "We're making great progress, wonderful, wonderful." You know what I mean? Having anxiety attacks, I'm breaking out all over. I don't know how I functioned in those days. I was a resident in psychiatry, and oh my God, it was awful.

So, anyway, the day of great terror came, and I couldn't breathe. I lay on the couch in sheer terror. He said, "What's going on? Do you have any dreams?" "Yes." I told him this dream. I said, "I'm in this dream, and there's some woman in the background, and I don't know if I was flirting with her or what, and then a lion jumped on me and began to kill me. And then the terror." I mean, I really had an anxiety attack on the couch; it was awful. He said, "What does a lion make you think of?" I said, "Jesus, I don't know." My mind was blank, blank. He says, "What's my name?" I said, "It's Lionel Ovesey." That was the name of my analyst. He was a professor at Columbia. Anyway, his name was Lionel. He said, "Who would the lion be?" And I realized he was the terrifying, castrating father figure. He was going to kill me for having Oedipal attractions to some female within his province, or something. So, people put down Freud as a—you go lay on the couch for a year or two and see what happens. So, this terror, this terror then arises and lies in wait.

How afraid should you be of your superego, your conscience, the judge—the savage, sadistic aspect? If you look at what your worst punishment for anybody would be, that's what it's saving up for you. If you think every sinner should be executed, then execution is what is waiting for you, because every one of your killer thoughts, there's a lot of people you wish dead. When you think of all the lifetimes you've lived and all the people you've killed and wished dead, I mean, there's a multitude, right? Oh boy. In a second you can think of a half-dozen people you wish dead already; you know what I mean? So, the superego says you're a murderer and you've got to suffer a penance, so suffering, then, is a way of trying to ameliorate God, offset his feared punishment by punishing yourself. So, we have to give up the worship of pain, suffering, sickness, and disease. You realize that the God of reality, you know, feels sorry for people, feels sorry for people. He doesn't feel sorry for people; it's just a way of speaking. The pain and suffering, then, is self-imposed, as the ego can be very vicious, huh?

When we see what the ego is capable of doing to other people, blowing them up 3,000 at a time, then you can't—it's not beyond credibility that your own superego can be quite savage. Therefore, I believe that *A Course in Miracles*, things that assuage the conscience—stop feeling guilty and seeing things as mistakes, seeing things as ignorance.

So, the shepherd, then, who is looking after your little lambs; your little lambs are susceptible. That's all the little parts of you that are vulnerable to attack by guilt, thinking that if you kill yourself and kill all your little lambs that God will be pleased. God of the Old Testament was pleased. They killed the little lambs, and the more innocent the little sacrifice. In South America and all these tribes, you see how sacrifice of the innocent was the way to assuage God, wasn't it? It had to be a virgin; it had to be a baby lamb. The slaying of innocents is how you pleased God. You see what a massive distortion of reality that is. That's a 180, right. Let's see if that's 180. "What we described is a 180: resist." [True.] It's a 180-degree reversal of the truth. And it holds sway over masses of mankind. And feels very threatened, very threatened by truth. Uh, okay.

Yes, and what can we blame on the human brain? That's a good question. I like blaming a lot on the human brain. It's one of my favorites. I mean, it's a very defective instrument. It doesn't remember to take the keys to the office. I have a new air conditioner at home, a little 650 BTU that goes through the wall. And it has a remote. You can set it for every other Tuesday, third Thursdays, and—if you're 20 years old, it's probably a turn-on. I finally have gotten "on," "off," I'm telling you. And I don't even touch the remote.

* * *

So, this next question has something to do with the brain. Well, there's a lot of questions, really, on this. How come we're born with a genetically defective brain to begin with? How come we're born with a consciousness that doesn't know truth from falsehood? Umm. We're born with an innate vulnerability in the nature of

Transcending the Intellect through Beauty | 55

consciousness itself, which is a priori to the mind and brain. Then you're born with a brain that barely knows left from right. What a lot of people think is very—erudition, you know, is jacks for openers. Amongst geniuses, those are just jacks for openers. Your genius thinks that's stupid. So, even the most advanced brain doesn't even know its you-know-what from its elbow. That's stupefying, isn't it? So, that's the vulnerability, that the shepherd has to take responsibility. All these innocent lambs within you that the shepherd has to take responsibility. All these innocent lambs within you are all vulnerable, easily programmable, impressionable. They've been programmed by the past, and now I would imagine it's one karmic—the evolution of the consciousness of mankind: "The karma of the evolution of the consciousness of mankind is what determines the kind of brain we inherit: resist." [True.] Okay. So, we've inherited it, it's really brilliant. It's also a genius. We've inherited an incredibly complex and very advanced brain as far as the rest of mankind-animal world goes. So, on the positive side, we've got an incredible computer that can do things that are really mind-boggling. Not only that, not just reason, but it can create such incredible beauty, such incredible beauty: the great operas, the great symphonies, the composers, the *Pietà*. I calibrated the *Pietà*. It was at 700, wasn't it? Yeah.

So, the mind of man is capable of incredible feats, of incredible beauty and great magnificence, great personal sacrifice out of love. So, its upside is that it's capable of taking you all the way to 1000. My presumption is, after 1000, you don't need it. In fact, it's probably a hindrance even below it. I don't want a brain after 1000, do you? No, I want to be rid of it. So, you might say, by the evolution of consciousness, mankind has earned karmically now the right to have a brain and all the benefits of the brain. But every gift is also a limitation, is it not? Just like the 400s are a gift as compared to the 200s, but it's already a limitation to get to the 500s. So, the human brain is certainly, I would say, useful to us at a certain point in the evolution of our consciousness, and not useful after a certain level. Not useful. Probably the human brain is quite a holdback at a certain level. You have to get rid of it. You have to transcend the human brain. So, that means we have to transcend physicality, and that's what heaven is about, isn't it? Heaven is going from physicality to more advanced consciousness, which the material physicality no longer plays an important element.

The evolution of consciousness then demands a comparable physicality, just as the dinosaur, the dinosaur was the perfect physicality to express consciousness level 70. Let's see what *Tyrannosaurus rex* was at: "*Tyrannosaurus rex*, we have permission: resist." [True.] "Was over 60." [True.] "Over 65." [True.] "70." [Not true.] *Tyrannosaurus rex* was at 70. Okay. We have people in the news that calibrate at 70! They make *big* news. You take a reptile and put him in a human body and let him loose with some bombs, and boy, you've got trouble.

So, the human brain, yes, is genetically defective. And that's one of the reasons we have to be merciful toward ourself and others. No matter how badly other people screw up, when the chips are really down, you really have to—you end up forgiving them. Why? Because you see they either couldn't—they either didn't know any better or they couldn't even if they did know. And that everyone is pretty much operating at the level of which they are capable, every instant. You can criticize anybody by holding their behavior up against the hypothetical, and everybody will fail, because you can—the hypothetical, you know, is a dime a dozen. You know, "He should've known better, he should've remembered that, he should've gotten an A, he should've remembered not to turn the corner that fast, he should've remembered to put the gas in before we left on the trip to Cincinnati." All those should-haves is the hypothetical. So, compared to the hypothetical, all of us fail. Nobody in this room can live up to the hypothetical. So, the hypothetical becomes the weapon, becomes a weapon, really, of hostility toward others. Nobody can live up to the hypothetical. So, we can only forgive people for being where they are at the moment. And hypothetically, five years down the road, they will remember to do whatever it is: remember to empty the garbage, but at this point, they don't remember to empty the garbage.

Fixation, obsession come out of the solar plexus. Addiction comes out of the solar plexus. Obsession to thoughts, obsession to rituals, obsessions and compulsions are primarily solar plexus. They are not "heart." I mean, that's not love, nor is it spiritual wisdom; neither is it hate—it's not coming out of the spleen—so it's really a fixation in the solar plexus.

CHAPTER 3

How to Reach the High Levels of Consciousness

How do we transcend the 500s to the 600s? The high 500s are unmistakable. In the high 500s, life becomes transformed. It happens to a lot of people who do the *Course in Miracles*. You see them go into this state. The miraculous becomes the commonplace. You think of a parking space. As you get there, a car pulls out, and there you are. You park right next to the Lincoln Center. You love everybody, you're in love with everybody. Everything looks beautiful. Everybody radiates. All the men look handsome, and all the women look beautiful. All animals are charming. Every street scene is like a French movie. It's just so! Central Park, Sunday afternoon, it's so beautiful. All the beautiful ladies walking with children, and everything is exquisite. The high 500s is a wonderful place to be.

And how do you get from there and beyond the 600s? I never asked myself the question. It happens of its own. It happens of its own. It can happen suddenly or slowly. You begin to—oh, I know how it works. You begin to get glimpses of it. You begin to get glimpses of it. As you get into the high 500s, it's not hard to get to the high 500s. I mean, it's hard, but it's not hard. You just do the *Course in Miracles* assiduously, pray up a storm, forgive everybody and everything, and be loving in all regards at every instant, and life transforms itself like that.

Then, the 600s I think, yes, they open, they begin to open, the window opens to it and then it closes. You're walking through the woods, and suddenly there's that absolute stillness and the present, there's a sense of a Presence. One knows one is in the Presence of God. It doesn't stay, though. At the beginning, very often it doesn't stay. And in the classic spiritual literature, the saint will bemoan how the beloved came and then deserted them, left them in despair; how they soared on the wings and then [makes sound] dropped. Because that which was infinitely loving now has the power to handle its challenge, its challenge: that which is not loving. So, it summons up that which is not loving in to be healed. So, that's the classic spiritual saying: "Love brings up nonlove." If you do a workshop on love, what you're going to be bringing up is all that which blocks the love, correct? Think about it: all of a sudden, all the people you hate come up. You do a class on forgiveness, all the people you . . . oh golly.

THE ATTRACTION OF OTHER DIMENSIONS: USE DISCRETION

What is the source of the esoteric? Don't forget, there are other dimensions in this—what we call "reality." This is only one of an infinite number of dimensions. What we call "our world," in reality, is one of an infinite number of dimensions. There is no limit to the number of dimensions. Classically they'd be called the inner planes, the celestial levels; the lower levels called "lower astral." Lower, middle, and upper astral. Celestial. Extraterrestrial. They've got different descriptive terms. We know that mankind has discovered over the centuries, by hallucinogenic drugs, by dreams, by shamanistic experiences, by vision, by the experience of others, et cetera, that there are multiple dimensions with multiple types of energies and beings in these multiple dimensions.

All we know is that the best spiritual teaching is not that they are unreal, but that you're not equipped to go there, and therefore, don't. You're not equipped to handle a Ouija board. You're not equipped. Nobody in this room is equipped to handle a Ouija board. Nobody here is equipped to handle that which is invisible and unknown, as intriguing and clever and glamorizing as it may be. There's nothing more intriguing than Master BlahBlah talking to you from somewhere, giving you the inner secrets of ancient mysteries. Oh, give me a break! Sedona is the home of ancient mysteries by Baba This-and-That being channeled by someplace. As you come into town, there's psychic readings on every billboard, right? So, it doesn't say it's wrong; it doesn't say it's bad; it just says you're not equipped to go there. You really are poking into realms of which you have no awareness of who it is on the other side. I had a spiritual teacher one time who says, "If you can't see or hear him in a body, avoid him." Because every spiritual truth that you ever need to hear in your entire lifetime has already been spoken by human beings in bodies. There's no great mystical truths spoken by Baba Somebody at midnight in the middle of the desert, waiting for the aliens to pick him up. You don't need it.

The basic things to reach enlightenment are really only a half dozen in number, aren't they? The willingness to forgive, the realization of limitations of the intellect, devotion to Divinity, the respect for the sacred, one-pointedness and fixity of mind, to transcend all obstacles, the willingness to be loving as a way of being in the world rather than some kind of emotional give-and-take: "I love you, now you love me, and if you don't love me, I'll be mad at you and kill you," et cetera—not an emotional give-and-take, but a way of being in the world. You only need to know about a half-dozen things. What do you need to know from Master Googleheimer on the other side? The ancient mystery of *what*? It's usually some symbols or numbers or strange name, you know, with a mystical, magical quality. So, this is the mystical, magical and its intrigue, which is one of the sheep you've got to watch, is glamour. It's all glamour. The glamour of the mystical, the glamour of the secret, the glamour of being initiated into the secret mystery and rituals of Humdedowas. And for another $5,000, you can become a Master Humdedowa in which we will give you the real secret symbols.

* * *

When I was reading the advanced theoretical physics, I learned a text. It's something about one of the variables that you deal with is one minus 300 billionths of a pixel or . . . so, I thought that would be a pixel a tiny, tiny moment of time. How small does a moment of time have to be before you're beyond time, huh? So, anyway, there's a lifetime—so, that was the meaning of this pirate's hat, because in that lifetime, I wasn't about to spend the money to bring those poor people back to port, I'll tell you. All my profit going down their throats, and . . . so, after the food and water. So, that's the ultimate of greed, huh? Greed, where even the life of others, much less their happiness or their comfort, is immaterial. And we see that in the daily news, right? That's every evening's newspaper.

[Q]: *"What about sensuality and sexuality as barriers to enlightenment? Should they be avoided?"*

Those are rather traditional things that every spiritual aspirant has to look at. Greed, money, work, fame, fortune, sensuality, sexuality, all the body's activities. There is a phase, there is a phase of self-detachment from all these things, in which one learns how to surrender, let go of cravingness in all of its forms. I did a tape on how to lose weight, in which I explained that in some detail. You let go: it's pretty much the same as letting go resisting pain, you know. You fall down and you twist your ankle. What you do is, you instantly don't label it "pain"; don't call it anything. Let go resisting whatever is, whatever the experiencing of it is without calling it anything. And the complete and total surrendering to the experience of whatever it is that's going on brings the pain from the ankle up into the aura. You can feel the pain leave your ankle, and you're surrounded by the pain. If you're surrounded by the pain that was once local, you know you're doing it right. Then, as the pain leaves here [the ankle] and becomes generalized, you can tell it's in your aura, you continue letting go resisting it. And by doing that, you disappear it. And within four or five minutes, you get up and walk away. Should have been in a splint, should have seen the doctor about a sprained ankle; instead, you get up and walk away.

So, it's somewhat the same with all the physical attachments, to eating and sex and the cravingness for excitement, et cetera. These are all things that're in the desire for money and fame and fortune and good looks and a great physique, and beauty and all these things. Um, they're all things that your willingness to surrender them to God—and I've discussed them in greater detail in *Eye of the I*, and perhaps again in the book *I*. You pretty much follow the same techniques you do with meditation, in which you let go resisting it. And as you let go resisting it, you see the magic. Each of these things has become imbued with a specialness. Each of these things has become imbued with specialness—a magical means of achieving something.

It isn't sensuality, it's the attachment to sensuality. It isn't sexuality, it's the attachment to it. Of course, Ramakrishna and many other spiritual warriors prohibit sexuality and such things—sensuality in any of its forms, and demand an ascetic, renunciate type of a lifestyle. I have nothing against that, and I myself have gone through that type of renunciation in which you leave the world and all of its—all that it values. It isn't just the things themselves; one thing I like about Alice Bailey's books is—the one on *Glamour*—that it isn't the thing itself; it's the specialness with which it has become imbued, the Hollywood extravaganza, and bigger-than-life blowing it up beyond that which it is. Each of these things then become special to us, and as we let go resisting them, let go of the attachment to them, the question always eventually comes up about one's willingness to surrender it to God. There's a method. . . .

So, it's the driven-ness of these things, that you become the slave, you're trapped by them. These are mainly solar plexus; ah, it isn't the sexuality, it's the attachment to the sexuality, the specialness of it, the glamour of it. All of these pleasures are transitory. How long does it take to eat a chocolate? You know, not very long. Bang, it's gone, right? An orgasm is an orgasm. It comes, it goes, and a second later, it's over already. And what you were expecting has left already. You know what I mean, you spent six months dreaming about it, and 22 seconds later, it's gone. For this you sacrificed all your hard-earned money. All those months out at sea, and this person says, "You pay me money now." Oh well, there goes 30 seconds. For that 30 seconds, people are willing to spend their whole lifetime in prison.

So, these things are traditionally addressed, and almost every spiritual group has its own approach to it. My own advisement is to follow the traditional way of nonattachment, no attachment, no resistance; to not resist it nor be attached to it. So, it becomes, it no longer runs you. Could it prevent enlightenment? Yes, it does at a certain point, certainly. And that's why Ramakrishna, you know, forbids his devotees to even touch money. No sex, no money. My only disagreement with that is that I don't think it's the sex or the money; I think it's the attachment to it. I think we calibrated money, and it's 200. And I think we calibrated sex, and it's 210 or something. So, it isn't like they have an intrinsic negative energy; it's the attachment to it. Let's see. Let's just do it for the fun of the audience, huh: "Money—we have permission to calibrate money: resist." [True.] "Money is over 200." [True.] "210." [Not true.] Yeah. Money is about 205, about the same as the CIA, the Internal Revenue Service. Peculiarly, all the big government agencies calibrate at 205. That means they're integrous, because the law demands it, I think. You know what I mean? But they're not gracious. Gracious is up in the 300s, you know. 205 would take you where? "You forgot to fill out the bottom line. Back of the line." I mean, they're doing their function. What was the other one? Money and sex, okay: "We have permission to do sex: resist." [True.] "Sex per se is over 200." [True.] "205." [Not true.] 205, yeah. It's a physicality procreative. Of course, we didn't ask about the emotional relationship in sex, which can be, of course, in the 500s. It can be, you know, the time at which you're really exchanging an adoration for each other in the 500s and the recognition of the Presence of God in each other, for which you're thankful. So, it can be a worshipful moment, a worshipful, and you thank God for the physicality and the chance to exchange love in that form, so sensuality and sexuality are not in and of themselves it's good to be beyond them, because when you reach a certain level of evolution of consciousness, you can be very powerfully attracted.

And don't just think because you're old and ugly that they don't happen. Old and ugly turns a lot of people on. For one thing, you're safe, there's no competition. Don't kid yourself; that passion can be very intense. But you notice that as you get into the 500s yourself, as you get into especially the high 500s, people are attracted to you like flies, and very amorously. They come on very amorously. There's almost an onslaught. People, they just fall in love with you. Well, at that level, you see, you're in love with everyone. So, what they're in love with is the reflection they're getting back of the recognition of their Self because of your lovingness. So, in your presence, they feel this intense state, which is spiritual love, but they misinterpret it as personal love. They think it's personal. No, it's not personal, but as you get in the high 500s, you find you're very attractive to people and, um, if you haven't transcended the temptation, you can fall. And there's a lot of well-known spiritual teachers with books calibrating reasonably well, but later on, later in their life, their personal calibrations fell down. And it was probably that this doorway was not guarded. So, as the shepherd of your sheep, that's another doorway you've got to watch. That the energy of lovingness is very, very attractive to people. And they will be attracted to you, and you will get very surprising propositions. At midnight in the zoo, the ape looks at you: "Hi, sweetheart."

[Q]: "At many spiritual meetings and seminars, there's more women than men, and yet, traditionally, it has been men who have been the great avatars, et cetera. Why is that?"

I never quite answered that before. Never questioned it before. I suppose it depends on the spiritual—it depends on the community, depends on the community. There are many communities where they're practically all men, especially the Middle East, et cetera; any congregation is almost 100 percent men. I don't know if they even let women in a mosque, do they? 100 percent men. So, it depends somewhat on the culture, depends on time, availability; it could be—we've never asked this before, whether the woman is more interested in the qualities, the qualities of life, whereas the man is more interested in the materiality of life. A good friend of mine right now is sawing wood and hammering things instead of here. Why is that? Just not into it. Last time, I said, "How come you're not there?" "Well, I wasn't into it, I was making a box." "When consciousness chooses the feminine dimension, it's seeking to evolve that aspect of its wholeness: resist." [True.] Yes. So, it's reaching out—let's see if we have the choice. "There is a karmically granted choice of gender: resist." [True.] Okay. "So, we could choose the woman; to be the woman because we realize that we're a hard-hearted materialist and we choose a feminine lifetime to learn nurturance." [True.] "Softness." [True.] "And the great feminine virtues." [True.] So, we want to own—who's that feminine goddess? Guan Yin. Anyway, it could be that the feminine lifetime is, then, to nurture those aspects which are not within the usual realm of testosterone. Testosterone is going down the highway with tattoos and a motorbike and a Harley Davidson. And why would he want to be at an airy-fairy seminar, you know what I'm saying? This is not the lifetime for that; he's still proving his macho and learning how to handle being a male, and what to do with all that testosterone besides having it kill you. Testosterone is the most fatal substance on the planet. It kills more people than anything else. I mean, all the wars—that's all testosterone. Martialing all that testosterone with all the flags and the music waving and bravado and being the hero, that's all testosterone. Testosterone kills more people than anything else on the planet. "In its biologic expression: resist." [True.] Fact. You look at Adolph Hitler up there: testosterone! Testosterone! Get that testosterone up with the flag! Deutschland über alles! They do it in Japan, they do it in China, they do it in Nanjing, they do it all over the planet, century after century. That's the rule of testosterone. When the consciousness level of mankind reaches beyond 500, they'll call ancient history "the ages of testosterone." Aggression, greed, murder, war, hostility, bombing. Imagine bombs in your shoes—I mean, is that demented, or what?

And yet, historically, the Great Avatars, et cetera, have been men. That's also correct. I think the reason is because the strain on the nervous system as you go up to really very advanced high levels, which are beyond this chart—as you go to the levels beyond 600, I think the strain on the nervous system becomes enormous. As you get up around the 7, beyond the 700s, it becomes, um, almost beyond the doable. The strain of the energy, the constant pain, the sort of agonizing feeling of hot wires being ripped out of your nervous system all the time. Any kind of negativity that you hold within your consciousness, it's just like you got put in the electric chair and they got it 10 volts below "kill," you know? And you've got to find out what that is; you've got to clear that with very intense prayer; and only with the help of the Holy Spirit does it even resolve. So, it's arduous. I don't think it's, uh, I think that's what it is, we'll just see. "The physicality of the man is needed to handle that kind of energy: resist." [True.] The physicality is really brutal. It seemed to perfect, uh, love and devotion, and then to go beyond that, into like the 800s and all, requires almost like a testosterone-driven, one-pointed ferocity. It's a ferocity; to grit and walk through the day with this agonizing, almost paralyzing pain; to act and behave normally and at the same time searching what it is in you that's out. Is it coming from out there? Is it coming from within you? Is it coming from your own karma? Is it coming from the collective? To try and track down the origin of it. So, I think that's what the answer is. It has nothing to do with femininity or masculinity.

It has to do with, I think, just the capacity of the physical body to handle shoveling tons of coal. There are women that can do it, but not statistically. They're not the great coal-shovelers of mankind, and, ah, why would anybody want to be? I mean, when you've got this kind of a body [his own], it means you're being really called to perfect certain things. And I think some people who deny gender are really denying the spiritual reality that this gender is supposed to be teaching them. And they are delaying their own maturation. Just like the man has to learn to overcome fear in the face of death, you've got to be able to walk into bullets.

If you don't walk into bullets, you just don't get over a certain level. For God and country, there comes a day when you've just got to walk into bullets, and that's sort of a testosterone kind of a thing, you know.

The woman faces the same thing, but differently, in the context of nurturance and childbirth, et cetera. She risks her life, over and over, and traditionally the women lost their lives frequently, childbirth fever, and died in childbirth. So, in my grandparents' day, our family Bible, you know, out of five children, three die; and the mother, then, eventually in the birth of the eighth child, dies. That was very, very common, so the great risk was the willingness to give one's life for nurturance, for continuance; out of compassion and love for one's children and the continuation of the race. So, it's just—to me, it has nothing to do with political correctness; it has to do with the obviousness of what the task would be in one form rather than another form, you know what I'm saying?

[Q]: "If individuals in high fives and sixes are holding up the consciousness of the rest of the world, what happens when they die? Does that level of consciousness remain within the world?"

I believe so. I mean, that's just my opinion. "The answer to that is yes. [True] "Yes, because it becomes part of the collective consciousness of mankind." [True.] So, see, every time you forgive someone or choose to forgive rather than hate, every time you choose mercy over revenge, this has not only a karmic consequence to yourself, but to the collective consciousness of mankind. You see, we saw that consciousness evolves—the calibrated level of consciousness of life itself evolves over time. And in this new book, I sort of track it from its appearance on earth and, you might say, the ooze. The ooze, what's the calibrated level of consciousness of the ooze? You know what I'm saying? The primordial ooze. And then out of that, the most important thing was that it doesn't happen as a chemical accident. The chemical, scientific viewpoint of evolution is that life started, you know, accidentally all these chemicals got together and

How to Reach the High Levels of Consciousness | 69

in the bright sunshine and bang, you had life. But that's a category error. Life is a totally different category from chemical-ness.

So, anyway, the level of consciousness of life on this planet has continuously gone up. The consciousness level of mankind has constantly gone up. Let's just redo the consciousness level of mankind at the time of Jesus Christ: "We have permission to do that: resist." [True.] "It was approximately 100: resist." [True.] The consciousness level of mankind as a whole was 100. Okay. "So, the impact of Christ on the consciousness level of mankind was to raise it dramatically: resist." [True.] "The impact of the Buddha on the consciousness level of mankind was to raise it dramatically: resist." [True.] "The impact of Krishna: resist." [True.] "The impact of all the great sages and gurus. [True.] "And saints." [True.] "The impact of Mother Teresa on the consciousness of mankind is uplifted: resist." [True.] "The impact of turning over the beetle helplessly lying on its back is to raise the consciousness level of mankind: resist." [True.] So, you don't have to be a great, recognized saint to profoundly affect the evolution of consciousness. So, we see it's gone up tremendously, tremendously, hmm?

All right, we've handled most of the questions. The question of suicide. I've never checked out suicide. We have permission—if we have permission to check it out. "We have permission to check out suicide in this audience right now: resist." [True.] Okay. I'll give you my intuitive understanding of it. The, um, karmic consequences of suicide are no different than that of the state of consciousness which led them to it in the first place: resist." [True.] "The physicality of it is irrelevant: resist." [True.] "So, if you commit suicide because you are in a state of grief at [level] 60, the only thing that happens is, you go out of body and you find yourself at 60: resist." [True.] Umm. So, it doesn't solve the problem. Now you don't have a physical body; you're in your spiritual body and you've still got the same dilemma, which may or may not be beneficial. Okay. I don't know. I don't want to jump with presumptions. "To not have a physical body could be actually an advantage at that point: resist." [Not true.] No. Hmm. "It's better to keep the physical body until its karma runs out: resist." [True.] Okay. "The time of death is already karmically set for this lifetime: resist." [True.] Okay. So, if you don't see it out, let's say you commit suicide three years before you're—let's say you're destined to die at 72, and you knock yourself off at 68. "You're going to have to spend three years on the other side: resist." [True.] "Until that karma's over: resist." [True.] "You're going to be a discarnate: resist. [True.] Yeah. Okay.

So, now you've got the misery that led you to do it, and the physicality, the karmic commitment; I don't understand that, because I've never researched it. A lot of this we're talking about is somewhat irrelevant, but . . . it is relevant, right. Spiritual questions come up. Because you have a microscope, all kinds of things you wouldn't have bothered with, now you've got to run and pull them out of the pond and look at them. So, to some degree we're doing that. But it is a natural question. "Praying for the individual who has committed suicide, we have permission to ask this: resist." [True.] "Is beneficial to them: resist." [True.] "It is beneficial, in other words." [True.] Okay. So, praying for the person who has committed suicide would be then beneficial and help them to overcome their guilt about it and all.

"The karmic consequences are due to the state of mind that led to the action: resist." [True.] "So, it's spiritual intention that sets the karmic cost or consequence: resist." [True.] So, it isn't the physicality's importance. So, if one did it out of hate, out of rage, out of despair, out of getting even, out of retaliation, out of, you know, skewering somebody else with guilt: "He made me do it." "You made me do it." No, that skewers them. Ha! So, the extreme hostility of that, so you're stuck with the karma of the extreme hostility which led you to try and skewer somebody else with a lifetime of guilt because you knocked yourself off, right?

So, we're still dealing, then, with the prices. The price and the quality of it all is occurring within the level of consciousness of which the physicality is then the acting out of it. It would seem, we'll ask this last and then we'll do it. "The karma's really no worse just because one acted on it: resist." [True.] "The karma's actually no worse: resist." [True.] "It's already worse. That's why you did it: resist." [True.] Uh huh. "In other words, the worseness has already happened already, that's why it's so. Suicide is merely the consequence of the despair and the self-hatred, or whatever it may be that led you to do it in the first place. So, it's again intention that seems to determine the karmic consequences.

* * *

"The karmic lifetime, the karma of the body is already set at birth: resist." [True.] "It's alterable: resist." [True.] "It's alterable: resist." [True.] "Alterable for worse: resist." [True.] You can alter it for worse. "You can increase the longevity through spiritual alignment: resist." [True.] Umm. "The lifetime would tend to be more healthy and extended just due to the energy of the spirituality: resist." [True.] Oh, I see, yes. Yeah, okay, because the energy. We have in the audience a doctor who did a study on the relationship between spirituality and survival from serious illness such as HIV, and very statistically accurate and very scientific, from an academic viewpoint. And it demonstrated that spiritual alignment and spiritual values—you can speak if you wish to.

Anyhow, the point of the study was that the longevity was related to spiritual commitment; that spiritual commitment tended to increase survival rate from any illness, and anybody who's been in a *Course in Miracles* group knows that. Because, in a *Course in Miracles* group, we've seen people with hopeless, advanced, fatal diseases, and they're still walking around, and some are at these meetings, in fact, who had a very slim chance of recovering.

* * *

Altruistic behavior and nonjudgmentalist: so, those are general spiritual principles, nonjudgmental and altruism, the thinking of the welfare of others—the opposite of the egocentricity of narcissism, which is the infantilism, which is the basis of criminality and all the things that hit the newspapers.

So, it's really maturation, then, to stop thinking about "me" and "my" wants and "my" desires, and blaming others, and accept responsibility. So, the altruistic person who turns over the beetle then has a much higher chance of surviving everything, and I think that's been proven with heart disease, heart attacks. There was a famous heart surgeon who wrote about it, did the first study on it, and those people who had a spiritual orientation to their life had a much higher survival rate from coronary artery disease and every other disease. They had a much better longevity. So, the answer was yes, you can increase the longevity of life in the body, then, by the sheer—what you change is the energy field in which it's being nurtured, yeah?

* * *

[Q]: "*How do you escape the attraction of the world and its doers of the world?*"

Well, you would not be attracted to it. Yes, and then there's a certain amount of spiritual work one does just out of one's relationship to the world in general. The ones in us who are glamorized by it, yeah. Most people are glamorized by it. The ones who are attracted to the sensationalism of it, the excitement of it, the drama. The society you're talking about is the ego projected "out there" for us to observe and learn from. So, the value, and I use social examples in my writings and talks because the ego projected out there is now dramatized on Channel 15 for you to witness, huh? And, um, so without being personally involved in it in particular, the more painless way is to witness it and learn from the observation of what is going on in society, and then you can see it within yourself and clear it. It's much easier to see it "out there." So, you can see the difficulties of positionality in the world and the price that is paid for it. This makes it somewhat easier to accept in yourself that this is a natural human proclivity. We're talking about softening up the superego before you start examining yourself with a microscope in detailed, very intense spiritual work, which people eventually get into, those that are really committed. Eventually, you get into rather intense meditations, some of which every single thing is examined with great intensity. By now, you're sophisticated enough to know that

that's not just a personal defect of "wonderful, wonderful" you, but this is the rubbing off of the nature of human society, so society is merely the projection of the collective ego, and so what we learn by watching the news and reading the newspaper—people say, "Well, shouldn't . . ." You know, there was a year—a period of time when that energy was totally prevailing, and there was no interest in the world or anything that went on in the world. Never read a paper, magazine. I didn't own a TV or radio. No idea what went on for 10 years or so. Um, one can conversely develop an aversion to the world.

So, to be perfectly balanced, there's neither attraction nor aversion. One is not repelled by the world and say, "Well, I can't watch TV, that's all disgusting stuff." Nor can you be attracted, so the perfect spiritual balance is neither aversion nor attraction. Because you have no aversion or attraction, you don't have to avoid it. To return to the world, you can't really have any deep aversion or attraction. It isn't a matter of being *de*tached, it's a matter of being *non*attached. If you're *de*tached from the world, which I did for a good 10 years, the world has no significance, importance, et cetera, huh. You're detached. You are not involved in the world; you have no involvement in the world. Whatever it is that you become is affecting the world just by the essence of that which it is, but there's no actions on your part in one way or the other. That's the perfect renunciate and the life of the ascetic. So, for some years, I was an ascetic renunciate. Never went anywhere, there was nothing to see, socializing was uninteresting. It was all irrelevant.

DETACHMENT AND NONATTACHMENT

Then—there's a difference between nonattachment and detachment. So, then there was a relinquishment of detachment as a positionality, as an aversion and avoidance. To see the world as a trap and therefore avoid it, which is the downside of being a renunciate. There is a time when your own spiritual reality has to be sufficiently strong that you can walk outside the cloisters and still remain that which you are. You can speak to strangers, eat food, and touch people, and either mate or not mate depending on the suitability of your lifestyle.

So, the detached person is a renunciate, avoids the world, and this can become itself a deterrent to enlightenment. If it's neither "this" nor "that," then you can participate, so the person who does return to the world does so on the level of nonattachment. It would not be safe if you're still attached, because it'll suck you right back in. And that's why Ramakrishna forbade his followers to touch—not have anything to do with sex or money, because the energy of the attraction was too strong, especially at a young age.

To be nonattached, then, means it's okay if it goes "this" way, and it's okay if it goes "that" way. If I see the parade, I will enjoy it, and if I don't see the parade, I won't—I won't miss it. Neutral is a very good space in which to work at that. Neutral, you're released from your attachments and your—your avoidance and attachments. You're pretty free. You can either stay or leave, it's okay. If we make it to the movie on time, we'll watch it. If we don't get there, we won't go. It's okay either way. You're not attached: you don't have to cry that you missed it; you don't have to get furious that your partner was fixing their hair and you couldn't get out the door in time, and therefore you missed the movie, or whatever. You know how life goes with people and daily bickering life: "Well, if you'd hurried up, we would have made it in time. Now they've changed the price, and now it's $4.50. If we'd gotten there when it was $3.50 . . ." So, life becomes this little, bickering trivia in which you're attached to winning and losing, and winning and losing face, winning and losing control.

So, then, at a certain point, one becomes nonattached; therefore, to win or to lose is really irrelevant. If the other person wins the argument, great. You won the argument. "Oh, you let him win the argument." Why not? It's fun letting people win. Did you ever do it? They cheat you out of a $1.20 and think you didn't catch them. I let him have the $1.20. Why not? You know what I mean? What difference does it make, you know? You're not attached to winning; you're not attached to losing. You're not afraid of winning and afraid of losing. You're afraid if you win that you'll get attached to winning-ness and get addicted, and that's what happens at the casino. So, a casino lets you win enough to get you hooked, yeah. Now, you'll keep coming back until you're cleaned out. So, that's the attachment.

The attachments, then, which we try to relinquish are really coming out of the solar plexus. Everybody thinks sex is the base chakra. No, it's the attachment. It's the solar-plexus attachment to that activity and what it does for your ego and your sense of satisfaction and your sense of aloneness, desirability, your self-esteem, so it's all the things that are piled into the meaning of that. So, we're attached to the meaning of things, and that's why we're addicted to certain activities.

So, the perfect practice, then, in a meditative, contemplative kind of a practice is neither attachment nor aversion. You neither hate it, nor are you addicted to it. You don't have to avoid it. If you're attached to things, then you have to avoid them. You can't have one piece of chocolate, because you know you'll eat the whole box. I remember when I finally got off chocolate. And I'd released . . . I'd let go of chocolate for a long time, and chocolate kept coming up. Finally, I completely lost any desire, thought, or appreciation for chocolate altogether. And, I said, "Wow! I'm off chocolate. I'm free of chocolate." I'd got unhooked from Diet Pepsi years past; now I have one can all day. So, all these things you get hooked on. I remember when I got free of chocolate; it was hysterical, because the very next night, the *Course in Miracles* group was coming out from New York and I had about 40 or 50 of them in the house, and they brought this huge chocolate cake! So, I didn't have to avoid it, because I wasn't going to get hooked by it again, so I could either have the chocolate cake or not have the chocolate cake. It was a great sense of freedom. I didn't have to avoid it for fear I would get hooked on it. And the same with Diet Pepsi. I finally got unhooked from Diet Pepsi, and now I can have a can or not have a can. There was a time if I left the house and there was no Diet Pepsi with me, I would turn around and drive five miles back to the house to get a Diet Pepsi. That's being hooked, right?

Now if I leave without a Diet Pepsi, I don't need one. So, the freedom to enjoy things, then, means being free from aversion or attraction. You do that through spiritual disciplines. The major ones, you don't have to go to a guru that's at 800 to get off these very important ones. You're looking at 200 to 2—you're looking how to get to 250. You don't have to have a world-famous guru or something, because this is spiritual practice to let go of your attachments and your aversions. And once you're free, then you're much quicker—you're much more free to move up more rapidly. So, I think these basic spiritual things, asceticism versus addiction, all these things are very important.

So, the 200s are extremely important, because it's really there that you go free. You see? The experience of God over here is freedom, huh? The experience of God, once you're over 200 over here. Where is God over here? Hmm. Well, he should be around 200, right here [points to several areas on board], about right in here. I don't know what happened to God as freedom. God-view as one of freedom is supposed to be in there. It must be on a different chart of it. About 210, you experience God as freedom. You suddenly own your own freedom, that you're free to choose. You're not hooked this way, and you're not hooked that way. And God is experienced as freedom. So, it's sort of an exuberant state of spiritual growth when you realize that God is not vindictive.

UNDERSTANDING KARMA IS A GREAT SPIRITUAL BENEFIT

To understand karma is a great spiritual benefit if you're a spiritual seeker. One of the difficulties with Western-style religion, et cetera, is, it doesn't really comprehend karma; nor does it realize its importance. It comprehends it in that it knows that negative behaviors in this lifetime will result in a negative consequence after you leave the physical body, so although it denies it believes in karma, it doesn't. What it really means when it denies karma is reincarnation. It means it doesn't believe in physical reincarnation. All religions believe in karma. Don't let anybody tell you differently.

The whole point of religion is the awareness and the responsibility that the spirit body is going to continue along after this physicality. So, if people were more aware in the Western world that every action has a consequence, a very profound consequence, and may have a very long-term consequence, then there would be greater responsibility. Responsibility. So, those cultures which are more sophisticated as far as their understanding of karma are much more aware that every action has a consequence. And it has a long-term consequence. So, we're going to do a whole session on karma. I forget the specific question she asked. Oh yes.

Because consciousness itself transcends many physicalities, many lifetimes—it goes on for eons, actually. Let's see: "We have permission to ask that: resist." [True.] "The consciousness had gone on for eons: resist." [True.] Therefore, we're talking about eons. This consciousness, the consciousness present in this room, has gone on for eons to reach this degree of evolution and complexity and consciousness and awareness. And there are many dimensions where no such thing goes on. There are many dimensions in which we are—already would be considered masters. And there are other dimensions in which we would be considered bumbling idiots. Let's see if that's so: "There are dimensions in which we, this group here, would be considered spiritual geniuses: resist." [True.] "We would be considered saints: resist." [True.] "We would be considered saviors: resist." [True.] So, compared to other dimensions, this group here, we're already extremely well advanced. "Compared to other evolved dimensions, we are bumbling idiots: resist." [True.] "Barely out of the cradle: resist." [True.] "And in kindergarten: resist." [True.]

So, if there's an infinite number of universes, and the infinite number of universes are expanding at an infinite rate, just the mathematical probability is that there are infinite numbers of universes more advanced than our own, and an infinite number of universes less advanced. That's okay, right? That's okay. Some are ahead; some are behind.

* * *

Now, if you take two apples, one, you don't know which is which, and I say, "Everybody, look at this apple," the whole crowd goes weak, and I say, "Look at this apple," the whole crowd goes strong, you know experimentally consciousness knows which one has the pesticide in it. It's been done blind on us, as well. When we were in Korea, we were handed two packages of green stuff, and she said, "Let's have the crowd calibrate them." You know, I didn't expect it, it wasn't on the program, she just came up with it. And, um, so we did. The one bag of greens, I think it was cabbage, made everybody in the crowd go weak; the [other] bag made them all go strong. And the one that made them all go weak was a pesticide, just like the apple experiment.

If merely looking at it, picking up on its aura can make you go weak, then what in the world would be the effect of ingesting that stuff for a lifetime? And what would be the effect on whole civilizations such as ours, where everybody's stuffed to the gozzle with pesticides? Scary, right? "We have permission to ask about this." [True.] We've never asked about this before. Umm. Oh, I get what it is. "The negative energy of the pesticide, compared to one's spiritual power, is extremely weak: resist." [True.] See, positive energies—because you're looking at logarithmic progression, the fact that you're coming to the person next door is so powerful that a little bad bit of pesticide doesn't really kill you. In other words, the negative is so weak—if it weren't for the fact that the negative energies are weak, mankind would not exist. We said that 85 percent of the people calibrate below 200. If their power was equal to this [above 200 on chart], the planet would have exploded millions of years ago. So, the negative effect of the pesticide is so weak, all right, so, it's like one-zillionth of an ounce of the negative. And just one loving thought as you pass an old lady on the street, you just sort of, your heart goes to her, has already negated all that. So, if you're very loving and pure in heart, you can eat a lot of pesticides. "That is a fact: resist." [True.] "It's just like smoking doesn't affect some people at all negatively: resist." [True.] Yeah. "It's because the chemical effect is so small, compared. That's why 15 percent counterbalances 85 percent: resist." [True.] Yeah.

So, pesticides do affect us negatively, because as we can demonstrate, and we can do it again in this audience, that merely looking at it makes you go weak. But that, of course, is a kinesiologic response, in which you're trying to decide whether that's a level below 200. That doesn't tell you how much *power* it has. It may make you go weak, but it may be very, very, very weak, huh? So, we don't have to be afraid of it, is what I mean. In other words, our positive energy is so powerful that we can handle a little negativity without going down the drain. It'd be a good thing, or none of us would be here. We'd all be killed by just breathing a couple of breaths of air or drinking the water.

So, perhaps some of the environmental fears are—they're correct but exaggerated. They're given far more power than they really have. Because man, if he changes his mind about something, can totally shift enormous amounts of energy and power. And the power of the negativity is too weak.

* * *

Just certain information itself, the reason I like to share it, is just the information itself already has a benefit. If you know that, um, if you know that you cannot experience your own physical death—it's not possible. You instantly leave the body just as the animal does, as the physical death occurs, and you are the witness of the physicality of it. Nobody can experience their own physical death. It's not possible. You'd have to be there, and you're not there anymore, so how could you experience it? You know what I mean? It doesn't even make sense. To know that is a relief. To know that the time of your departure is already preset is a relief. Why worry about it? You don't have to worry about it, it's all preset. You might as well have a good time and enjoy yourself. If that's set, the calibrated level of consciousness is already set at the time of birth—you're already born at whatever you start out at. So, you don't have to feel guilty that, you know, you're not a genius. If you're with an IQ of 82, you're going to learn what you can at 82, because that's what you're supposed to be doing at 82, is learning how to spell. So, we accept that which we are. We say—we give thanks to the Lord that these are many things that are taken out of our hands, that they would be a great burden to us. And we thank Thee, Lord, for taking on the responsibility of our life, our human life, our appearance, our departure, and our ultimate destiny. Ohmmmm. Ahmmmm. We did the *Ohm*, and we saw that it calibrated much higher than pronouncing it differently. Consequently, we'll go, Ohmmmmmmm. Ohmmmmmmmmmm. And I thank you all.

CHAPTER 4

Transcending the Mind through "No Mind"

Today we're speaking on "no mind." And what there is to say about it, I can't think of. As she was pinning me up with all these things, I thought, the best way to become a good Christian is to be a Buddhist. There's a wonderful Buddhist community here, and a wonderful Christian community. And I always say, the way to become a good Buddhist is to be a good Christian, and vice versa. Because the essence of truth remains the same throughout the ages. And the novelty of the lectures we give is that a means of ascertaining truth, which was not before available, became available, and we then had a way of going back over spiritual and religious history throughout all of time, and reaffirming and discovering and clarifying many things. So, the books that we've been writing have to do with clarification, because spiritual reality is difficult to comprehend by the mind, and what's been written about it over the centuries has sometimes been misleading. Plus, there's a great deal that is erroneous and was considered to be spiritual literature. And we recommend that exercise where you go through your spiritual library, and everything that makes you go strong, you put it in one pile. Everything that makes you go weak, you put in another pile, and it's quite an amazing discovery—sort of weed out the poppycock. And what's the reason for that? It's because the mind just loves things that are mysterious, magical, occult, and ooh, woo sounding. And we get trapped by that, the intrigue of the magical and confusing the magical with the miraculous—two different realms.

So, we're really going to summarize what we've said so far. The series of lectures has really been preparatory to become acquainted with the nature of the ego and therefore to disassemble it. And we started out to do so the very first lecture, which we repeat every time. I want you to become aware that everything is happening spontaneously of its own. Everything here is spontaneously becoming what it is, and it's not being "caused" by anything. There is no "cause" within reality. The subject of nonduality, which has to do with "no mind," which has to do with no mind . . . The most basic understanding, and it's the reason it was the very first thing we spoke of, is the realization that causality itself is an illusion because the entire ego is based on the notion of causality. To transcend the notion of causality actually is quite a high comprehension. To transcend causality: "We have permission to ask this: resist." [True.] "Is over 996." [True.] "997." [True.] "998." [True.]

The ego is based on the concept that everything is being *caused* by something else. And that nothing really can exist therefore as it *is*, without being caused by something else. So, we repeat this each time, because to merely hear this, to merely know it, begins to undo its power. Because Creation, That "Which Is" manifests by virtue of the grace, by virtue of the grace of its source, which is the Creator. The unmanifest becoming manifest is Creation itself, the Source of all existence. There's only one power in the universe sufficiently powerful to account for existence itself. Each of us comes in thinking, "Well, I came into this world due to the genes of my parents," and because of the whole long sequence of genes is how we account for our present existence of the human race. As you're aware, creation is continuous. By grace, each instant, everything is becoming the fulfillment of its infinite potential. Everything is manifesting the power of creation by virtue of its Source. To acknowledge God as the Source of one's existence is a very, very powerful statement, and already takes consciousness leaps ahead. It's the source of power of the United States Constitution, which calibrates at 700, the highest in the world. By virtue of the Divinity of our Creator, out of that comes all rights, all rights of our citizens—not by vote, not by the power of politics, not by armed might, not by the force of a dictator, but by virtue of the Divinity of our Creator. That puts it at 700. Consequently, to try to remove that acknowledgment is not really in the service of one's own spiritual advancement or that of others.

Which brings us to one of the great difficulties of mind, and that is, you understand that mind works on content within a certain context, so we can shorten this whole trip of transcending mind, which we've tried to do throughout all of these lectures by disassembling it. And then we finally get to the core of something we can address. We all do letting go, we all do surrender, we all try to become nonattached to the world, let go aversions and attractions. And this is sort of continuous. It's also sort of a continuous meditation. It's really a contemplation. And there's a borderline between contemplation and meditation, in which you go about through the day with a certain equanimity, because as each thing comes up, you let it go; as it comes up, you let it go; as it comes up, you let it go, and just as we were leaving this morning, the kitty was missing; we're ready to go and the kitty's missing. Argh! The screen is open. Where is kitty? Oh God. So, it's interesting what the mind does at that moment, you know. It instantly detached from this kitty. All kitties are kitty-ness. And let go, for kitty-ness will re-present itself. So I said to Susan, "I affirm the positive: not that he's lost, but kitty always returns," which is a fact, and so she called Brock and said kitty is missing. Brock, he lives right near us; Brock went to his front door, and the kitty walked in. I mean, is there a problem? What is the problem? Kitty had no problem, sat down and purred, and was fine.

Everything that presents itself to mind, everything that—every little tool in the mind, every mechanism in the mind, we're dealing with content within context. To see all things as content, within usually an unstated context, is one way to quickly transcend mind. Mind focuses on content. The content is a statement of fact: "Kitty is missing," whatever. The content then triggers all kinds of emotional reactions, as you can see. "How can we go without kitty?" "I don't know what might happen to kitty." "The dog might get kitty." "The raccoon might get kitty." I went outside; sure enough, there was a big raccoon out there, skunks all over the place, coyotes who eat kitties, dogs. I mean, what are we, living in a zoo here? What is this? A wildlife zoo. All right.

So, the only thing you can do is surrender kitty, who is the content, to God, who is the infinite Context. And you formalize it by asking the Holy Spirit to find kitty. Holy Spirit was pretty quick this morning, a couple of minutes. Constantly dissolving content into context. All right. You see that almost all human error, 90 percent of human error is the failure to define context. Every night on TV we see, you know, a lot of shocking examples of literally looking at content and completely ignoring context. Because the truth of content depends completely on context. In fact, without context, content has no meaning at all. So . . .

Last night on television, there was some woman who was abysmally abused in the airport going through the examination line, and night after night, there is some poor creature there who's had her wooden leg removed and stripped naked, and night after night, there's an atrocity. Atrocities are committed by these people who check you out at the check-in counter. Totally missing the whole point, isn't it? I mean, the total missing of the intention of the whole thing is so drastic. If you're looking for black people, you don't stop all the white people on the street, do you? If you're looking for white people, you don't stop all the black people on the street. If you're looking for a man, you don't stop all the women, do you? And so, you see an absurdity, an absurdity where the context is totally lost. That people should not be harassed because of their race is the intention, and then its application becomes the opposite, becomes an absurdity, you see. Oh Lord. . . .

So, context transforms everything. When the fire danger is high, which it was at the last lecture—in a fire danger, we had huge fires all over Arizona, you're not allowed to go camping. You can say, "Well, it's my right. I pay taxes, I have a right to camp." Haha. But the context is changed: extreme fire danger. So, I just cite, then, as examples we can see every night on television where ignoring context, you see the absurdity of what would otherwise be sensible content. Nobody argues that people should not be discriminated against by virtue of race and culture, whatever. And then what happens to that truth? That truth then becomes actually its opposite, it actually becomes its opposite. I think these people at the check-in counter are on a combined program to destroy this thing because it's so absurd, so they take it to the other extreme to try to get it overturned, because, you know, stopping every little old lady who has a steel pin in her hip is not the way to find terrorists. That's not the way to find them, actually. And mathematically it was discovered that the chances are diminished by 6,000 to 1 by following our current check-in style and diminishes its effectiveness by 6,000 percent or something. If we stopped all that, our chances of finding a real shoe bomber would be 6,000 times higher. The whole thing is absurd, is it not? Can you imagine a shoe bomber, and he's going to go to heaven and taking all these innocent people with him? The way you get to heaven is, you wear bombs in your shoes and you blow up all kinds of innocent people. And these people that buy this, that's truth. So, the extent to which truth becomes mangled when content is taken out of context . . .

It's possible, and of course it's a big problem in our current society, maybe for 50 million years or 40 million years or whatever, because *Homo sapiens* is really a transitional life-form. *Homo sapiens* is transitional. We like to look at *Homo sapiens* as a crowning glory of evolution, above the monkeys and all those things below us, you see. In modern man—in our own fantasy, modern man is the most advanced creature that could be, really. We'll soon be going to the moon—no, we went to the moon; we'll soon be going someplace, always, to show the advancing superiority of the human race, huh? Let's see, what do we call current man? *Homo sapiens*, right? *Homo sapiens*, yeah? "*Homo sapiens*, we have permission to ask this: resist." [True.] "*Homo sapiens* is a transitory genus: resist." [True.] Transitory; we're not permanent. Neanderthal man wasn't permanent. Cro-Magnon man wasn't permanent. *Homo erectus, Australopithecus,* is that right? All those folks back there. Cousins. All those cousins back there were transitory. And we are transitory. This couldn't possibly be the ultimate possibility of evolution. Absurdity which you watch on TV every night: strip-searching a little old lady with the steel pin in her hip. That can't possibly be the ultimate evolution of consciousness, huh? I'm glad we got the answer we got. What if we had got, "This is it, folks"? Oh wow.

So, how far can you go with an animal body? I mean, you've got an animal body, and you've got this consciousness. I mean, how much farther can you go with it, you know? We've got the Olympics, to see how far you can strain it. What can you get out of this combination of things here? I've lost interest in eating years ago, or any other activity that it does. It entertains me, and without it, my wife would be forlorn. And so, I say, well, keep it, 'cause without it, she'd say, "Where are ya?" People get attached to the body, so it's inevitable; it's part of the animal's nature to be attached to the body.

So, we trace the evolution of consciousness from its origination up through the evolution of life-forms on the planet. In the book *I*, there's a dazzling chapter on it. Tracking the evolution of the energy of life as it evolves over millennia, over hundreds of millions of years. And of course, as it does, it goes up through the animal kingdom, and as it goes through the animal kingdom and we have a physical brain with all kinds of animal parts in it, which still fire off, unasked. And so, we're where evolution takes us. The animal has evolved to the point where it can think, and now it's becoming spiritually conscious, and then we mark, that in late 1980s the consciousness level of mankind went over 200 for the first time. In the book, I said, "That marks the appearance of a new genus: *Homo spiritus*." Let's see if that's a fact or my fantasy. Could be my fantasy. "That is a fact: resist." [True.] Okay. *Homo spiritus*. Okay. We can't ask about the future.

Homo spiritus. The nervous system of mankind can only handle calibrated energies up to about 600. To push it over 600 is—you've got to be really weird to do that. It's extremely arduous.

Anyway, to evolve through into lovingness as the way you are in the world, 500, we calibrate that 500. Lovingness is the way you are, it's what you've become. 540 is unconditional lovingness, not as an emotion, not as something that goes between yourself and help that which is out there, but it's what you've become. Like the hummingbird becomes his humming. He just does that because that's what he is, you know? So, he doesn't aspire to anything; it's just what the hummingbird is. What the hummingbird does is just, [hums] hummm, and it sucks nectar and likes flowers. It does that because that's what it *is*. That's what it is.

The calibrated levels of the 500s then indicate that that's what you have become. It's a way of being in the world. It then eventually becomes the context of your life. The context of your life then becomes the energy field of lovingness itself, because you've let go all the obstacles. One of the obstacles is the mind, as we all know.

Under 400s, ah, well, under 200, let's see. We have animal problems. The reason we trace the evolution of consciousness is because when you see its origin, you stop feeling guilt, shame; you stop hating it, you stop cheering it. You just say, "Oh, that's my little animal." It's good to give your little animal a name. Somebody cuts in front of you: "Yousonofabit"—there goes Kookoo again. Inside of yourself is this invisible animal named "Kookoo." Kookoo, very Kookoo! From a human viewpoint, it's Kookoo. From the Kookoo's viewpoint, you don't make much sense. "You let the SOB in front of you. What's the matter with you? Aren't you a man? Let's be aggressive. Let's get over our inhibition about asserting ourselves." "All right! Take that, you SOB!" Give him the finger as you go by, hurrah!

I discovered the finger late in life. It was a joyous moment, joyous. It happened in Sedona. I was brought up in a very dignified, traditional, high Episcopal, Protestant lifestyle. We didn't use any vulgarities, crude language. And the naughtiest thing my sister and I did when we were kids—we had pianos all over the house, because my family were all musicians. Everybody was gone. She sat at the top of the piano, I sat at the bottom. She hit the keys—we were both about this big—and she went, "Pew!" and I went,

"Stink." "Pew!" "Stink." Man! We were so wildly bad! We used those bad words and weren't allowed to use vulgarities. So, that was being awful.

So, inside ourselves there's an animal. Oh yes, I was telling you about Sedona. So, overt expressions of hostility, anger, vulgarities—cultured people don't do that in the best circles, and we lived in the best circles. In the East I belonged to the most ultimate club, and such things were not. . . . So, here I am in Sedona, and I go out; turns out I was going in the entrance, so I was wrong to begin with. So, this woman comes in and she blows her horn at me and was very, very angry, and all of sudden, out of my animal Kookoo, I went. I did it! Transcended hundreds of years of culture, education, M.D.s, Ph.D.s, master's degrees, the ultimate social club—it's so exclusive, the world hasn't even heard of this club. You actually have to live in that enclave to even hear of the club. So, anyway. It was victorious; it was a wonderful moment. I discovered that within myself. Take that! Wonderful. So, you can love your Kookoo side, huh? There he is [low on MoC], Grrrr! So, I love this beast in me. He's really a lion, a tiger, grrrrrrr! And I love him. I love him! Here's my guilt monger. Here's the old monk, beating himself with chains, and he's got a hair shirt; he kneels on his bare knees until they bleed. Have you ever done that? Oh, you've done it in lifetimes. How many people have done it in previous lifetimes? Oh, a lot of you. All kinds of people have done all those things. Here, you put yourself out of the decent human relationships. We've done all these things down here.

So, we don't have to pretend they're not there. Why would we pretend? We can pretend they're not there out of shame and guilt. But without that animal-ness, you wouldn't be walking around, huh? They stick you; you bleed. That's the animal bleeding, you know. Right? So, the way you disappear the dominance of the animal in you is, you own it. Love it. I love my kitty. If I squeeze my kitty too hard, he'll scratch—no, he won't, because I took his front claws off. Inside of me there is a meannn critter. No, actually I didn't do it out of meanness. I did it to save the cat's life, because I would have thrown him across the room and he would have died of a fractured skull, involuntarily. He used to do this when I was taking a nap. And I'm always cold, I'm always cold all the time. In the wintertime I've got about six layers of stuff, and these claws went right through into me, and I picked the cat up and I threw it. So, I said, "Kitty, we've got to do something here. I had to get my wisdom teeth taken out, and you're going to have to get your claws . . ." I mean, it's just life, you know.

So, down here the problems are emotions, and spiritually oriented people go into consternation when they find out what's hanging out in their unconscious. If you want to know what's hanging out in your unconscious, read Freud. He's right. Every negative thing that you can think of is in your id. It's in there. It's in your id, and it's repressed because you have a conscience which Freud called the superego. You feel guilty about it. "I don't want to kill anybody, it's the last thing I'd ever do." Anybody who says that is a killer; watch out. Of course the unconscious wants to kill people. When somebody cuts in front of you, you'd like to kill 'em. So, after a while, you see, as you admit your animal by owning him, learning to love him. . . . How do you get an animal trained—is loving them and training them, right? Not by locking them in a box and pretending they don't exist. So, your animal's legitimate.

If it wasn't God's will that you have an animal body, you wouldn't have one, right? So, the nature of creation is that we evolve it through. So, we have the remnants of animal-ness. The spiritual people call that "ego." This part, then, has to do with negative emotions. When we start to get okay with it, we have the courage to look at it, face it, and we start going into integrity. These energies here in the low 200s have to do with attitudes, letting go of positionalities, the willingness to dig in, the willingness to deal with the problems of being a human and accepting it so that we arrive at some kind of peace about it. So, at first, we're dealing with animal-ness, right, in our evolution. We're dealing with all this animal-ness [below 200]. Greed, of course, greed is what runs the big corporations and hits the headlines all the time. So, if you don't get over the solar plexus, you end up on TV, that the world is teed off that you took $500 million and left all the widows out there just penniless, and the world takes a dim view of that. So, the solar plexus takes off with you. . . .

So, above 200 has to do with learning, doingness. This has to do with—in Sanskrit, called *rajas*—action, activity. These are the builders of the world; 200 and up builds the world. Designs the factories, sets up the commerce, runs the trains, the airplanes. When we get up to the 400s, which is the dominance of life by logic and reason, in which education becomes profoundly important. In our culture, education is probably the most important aspect that we strive for. People go without all kinds of things for education. And, so, they go without all kinds of things to develop this, because the 400s are far more powerful than all this.

You can be mad as all hell and nothing really happens in the world, but you get up to reason and logic, and you redesign the whole highway, elect the officials you want, learn how to raise money, and politics, et cetera. So, the 400s are very powerful. And groups such as this one here are usually quite erudite. Compared to the rest of the world, this is an extremely erudite group. I mean, this is probably one-tenth of one percent of the world's population here, or less. It gets up to the 400s, and then in the 400s becomes interested in spiritual reality and begins to study it, begins to read all the great teachers. So, inspiration together with the intellect, then we find ourself in the 400s. So, the reason and logic, then, serves us well; it increases our power enormously. You can manipulate with a computer what would take 100,000 people a month to accomplish, hmm? In one second [snaps fingers], you can accomplish a great amount of work—in one split second—that a large percentage of a whole subcontinent, if they worked all day, every day, couldn't accomplish what you can accomplish, because symbols now become the great power.

So, reason and logic, which is in the 400s . . . The 400s are very, very powerful. They dominate the world right now. They dominate civilized society. The 400s, which then give you the intelligence to begin to see the truth of spiritual reality, the capacity to read, and value a spiritual education, now becomes—as you get to the top of the 400s, what was an asset now becomes an obstacle.

The 400s got you here, and now you're stuck with it. You're stuck with reason and logic and the constructions, because the mind takes positionalities. Out of that positionality, it automatically instantly creates duality.

* * *

So, in this lecture, our purpose is to see how can you transcend duality. The classic pathway, let's say, of Zen and various types of Buddhism and monastic types of meditation transcend the mind altogether, to experience another reality directly. And the various techniques about which I've written, and about which we've lectured and which all of you have studied . . . Certain realizations seem to potentiate that transformation that transcends the limits of the ego, so that instead of being an obstacle, it begins to serve you. Certain things, merely to hear of them already begin to, hmm, accelerate one's progress. If we say, nothing is—it's not possible for anything to cause anything else, everything is manifesting its infinite potentiality by the grace of Creation which is continuous: just that knowingness, that thought is already powerfully transformative. Let's see what the calibration of that thought is. I don't know: "As just spoken, we have permission: resist." [True.] "That is over 800." [True.] "850." [True.] "900." [True.] "920." [Not true.] The thought has the power of 920. That's the level of the truth of the thought. To merely hold that in mind, then, and to give it a certain reverence which we give to all Truth, then empowers that thought, which then sort of goes through your mind and [makes clipping sounds] cuts off a whole bunch of circuits. See what I mean? You, like, let it loose in this syncytial nightmare we call the brain, and it runs around on its own now and begins to disconnect switches. Because causality is not what accounts for "That Which Is"; then the mind automatically increases, expands its context, and begins to try to sense what it is.

All that we look at, then, is content. As you mature spiritually, you look less and less at content and look more and more at context. One begins to sense the field in which that thought is occurring. Again, you see, as you expand context, the context itself is limited by certain definitions. And you start letting go of the definitions. Eventually context becomes the Infinite Presence out of which the entire universe manifests—the Unmanifest manifesting itself as the manifest, which is the source of Creation in which we experience existence. The only possible source of existence is Divinity Itself. And out of this awareness—and moving up into the heart, where you begin to see the beauty of all that exists, because you stop thinking about it. When you stop thinking about it, you see the beauty of all that exists.

So, through the doorway of beauty and the letting go of thinkingness, because you're branching out your awareness to the field instead of the content of the field, one experiences the Presence, the Presence of Divinity, which manifests itself as existence. There is nothing that has the power to bring about existence from nothingness. Once you take away causality as an excuse, a rationalization . . . Causality is the ego's last hold. The Buddha defined it as the "law of dependent causation," or something. And that law is at 996. What we're talking about today calibrates at 998. Nothing is *causing anything*.

Everything is being continuously sourced by a continuous Presence which gives it the power to manifest its infinite potentiality as that which it is. So, the hummingbird, as his wings go down, does not cause the next thing of his wings going up—which does not *cause* the next thing of his wings going up. The source of this wing movement is exactly the source of this wing movement, is exactly the source . . . it is a continuous source. And what the source does is empower the potentiality to become manifest as existence, which we then witness as life. Is that clear? Of course it's clear. Everybody here gets it and understands it. Some people don't realize that they understand it, that's all. And I want to remove that obstacle. Everybody here *knows* that, or you couldn't exist. How could you exist unless you came into existence? I mean, it's a stupid question, isn't it? The source of existence, obviously, is how come you exist, yeah. It's like kindergarten thinking and too much for advanced intellectual people like us to "get." Yeah, the only way you can be here is because you *are here*. Oh wow! Let's see if that's a good one, Susie. Let's see: "That is over 998." [True.] "999." [True.] So, that is what they need to know. All right. So, that knowingness is present within you, latent, but after this morning, no longer latent. It's vibrating in everybody's aura right now. So, that knowingness is there forever.

The pathway of duality, then, is called "no mind." No mind. Um, in this experience which occurred within, it wasn't called "no mind," because there was no mind to call it "no mind." I learned about "no mind" many years later—because to reacquire mind is a project. It is not easy. And most people don't have any mind left, leave it that way, and we don't hear from them again, which is, frankly, the best advice, I think. The best thing to do when you go into a bliss state and realize that Love, God, Oneness, and "That Which You Are" are One and you're immobilized in that state: resist the temptation to reactivate the body; that is my advice. However, you may have had a prior karmic commitment about it, which may pull you back in.

So, the condition of "no mind." If it's the Silence that teaches, then how can you teach silence when you're talking? Oh yes, this had to do with an interview with Ramana Maharshi. Maharshi, in response to a question, had said that the teaching happens as a matter of silence. So, this person wanted to know how that could be. It's because the silence is always present. Your talkingness does not eliminate the silence; it distracts you from it. But the Silence of the energy of the field itself transmits. Everyone within this room is sharing that. We're all sharing it with each other because we're all just One, and so the oneness of that knowingness is sufficient. So, while Ramana Maharshi is chattering to you about something because he's got to amuse this visitor—because visitors are very verbal; you've got to say something to this guy who came all the way from Cleveland to see him. So, Ramana looks at him, and he's busy eating his porridge on his palm leaf or something, and that was the transmission. Then the seeker says, "It looks like you're unhappy." He said this; Ramana said that. But that had nothing to do with what happened, huh. So, "no mind," then, is silent.

"No mind" is really nothing but the realization of the ultimate context of one's own existence, so the content, the content, then, is your existence. We've said that there's content. Meaning comes out of content, but only within a context. So, then, let's take as a proposition for the content your own existence, and what is the ultimate context of your own existence, huh? I don't agree with Ramana Maharshi—he came up in questions in the office. I saw some visitors this week because of his instruction to ask all that's continuously as a continuous contemplation, "Who am I?" I don't agree with "Who am I?" because "who" makes you look for a pronoun. It looks for a—see, it's already a limitation. A "who" is a limitation. So, you're looking for a "who," you know. And there isn't any "who." There isn't no "who" there. You're looking for a "not who." You're looking for a "not who." If you find a "who," that isn't it.

You're looking for a condition, a "what." The sense of Self within is a "whatness," it's an "is-ness," it's a "condition-ness," and it's also the most powerful sense of "I" that can exist. It is "I," but beyond the pronoun *I*. So, I'm always afraid of people who say, "Who am I?" They're looking for a pronoun. A pronoun of Self, definition of "I," and it's going to take them right back into the ego's definition of who you think you are.

The infinite stillness, behind whatever sounds we hear in the room, is your Self. Without the infinite stillness of your Self, you wouldn't be able to hear anything. Without the infinite context of nonform, you would not be able to experience form. Because of the voidness of the Presence, one experiences form, experiences existence, is aware of what the mind is up to. So, we don't want to be scared of mind. We want to handle mind the same as we did the animal. We love mind. It's not our enemy. It took evolution billions of years to develop this incredible thing here, which I now—because I want to realize the Presence of God, now becomes an obstacle. Got all the way to Mars, and now how do you get off the place? Here we are, folks. Without this, you'd never get to Mars. What do you do once you get to Mars? You try to figure how to get off Mars, that's what you do. You got enough gas left, Susie? I don't think we can get off this place. All right.

So, whether a thing is a deterrent or a tool, whether it's an asset or a curse all depends on how you look at it. If you love all this stuff here, in the middle area of the Map, you're going to have a good time with it. I had a whale of a good time giving that lady the finger—I mean, it was wonderful! I just found that beast in me, and he just, wow! I can be completely detached, you know. This morning, the cat's missing. Release on the cat, lots of cats, another one will come along. One cat's a dime a dozen. Well, one time we did that, I think, in front of the audience. We'll just do it again, take care of the kitty. Hm hum: "We have permission to ask about the orange kitty: resist." [True.] "There's only one orange kitty in reality: resist." [True.] There's only one orange kitty, and its attractor field exists within the animal realm, and it manifests serially as thousands, millions of orange kitties, but it's all the same orange kitty. Same orange kitty, just back in the same body. Same—you know, all orange kitties have the same nature; they're all the same. So anyway. I let go of orange kitty, and so that was here, above 200. The willingness to do that and accepting that maybe kitty is gone, and reason tells me there's been a lot of kitties. And I loved that kitty, and I loved the next kitty, and the realization of all the truth of this brings me joyfulness and peace. And in that joyfulness and peace I said, "Holy Spirit, we ask for a miracle." And Brock said, "Your kitty's down here." So, there you are. You go through the whole—whoosh, all the way down, all the way through the whole thing. So, you transcend the limitation of content by energizing your awareness of context. Out of the context, energizing the context arises the miraculous. The kitty appears, and I walk up to the bathroom door, and she opened the door, and she said, "There's kitty." So, in the sequential world of perception, then, that was the moment of crying with happiness, eh? Everyone was happy.

If you hold in mind, "Kitty is lost," now you're giving power to "kitty is lost," you understand? No, kitty's not lost, kitty always returns home, and if kitty doesn't return home in this physicality, orange kitty will get impatient on the other side and energize in

96 | SPIRITUAL POWER AND INTEGRITY

another orange body and be right back. When you hear it purring, it's going to be the same kitty. Let's see if that's so: "We have permission: resist." [True.] "It is the same kitty: resist." [True.] It is the same kitty. I told you that. Somebody there had a doubt, now you made me go do this! And of course, we've done the lovingness of the kitty's purr. Everybody's seen that.

Anybody not seen the calibration of the kitty purr? We love the kitty purr. We'll just do it for those who've never seen it: "Kitty's purr is over 480." [True.] "490." [True.] "500." [True.] "502." [Not true.] Kitty's purr is 500. Isn't that miraculous? In the world where they strip-search old ladies and take a baton and whack on their steel hip replacement, the cats have a heart at 500? Would orange kitty do that to her? No! Orange kitty wouldn't make a poor, old lady strip-search and bang a baton against her steel hip to make sure that's not a bomb in there!

* * *

So, we don't have to get depressed about the human condition, because we got that this is just a phase. This is—you know, we're like Cro-Magnon man. We're the current expression of where this line of evolution is going, so we can take that, then, instead of feeling sorry for ourselves. Okay, we could accept that, be willing to serve. In a way, then, as a species we are serving God in being that link in the evolution of consciousness. No, we're not the link; we're the *expression* of the link. The evolution of consciousness goes on in the nonphysical domain. And then sporadically expresses in the physical. That's why evolution is sporadic. See, evolution—the monkey doesn't get smarter and smarter and become a Cro-Magnon man and then a Ph.D. at NAU, you know. No, he gets off the bus here, and then the main line goes to the next bus, so, we come off like this.

So, here we are, *Homo hystericus, Homo absurditus, Homo ludicrous, Homo patheticus, Homo funniness*! Hysterical. I think humans are funny. Anyway, you get up through here, you see. So, our job, then, our job—so, as we evolve our consciousness, we're doing it for all that follow us. If it wasn't for Neanderthal man, maybe we wouldn't be here. I don't know. I never asked that. Let's see: "We have permission to ask that: resist." [True.] Umm. "They served as a link in our own evolution." [True.] "So did Cro-Magnon man." [True.] "All these people, all these ones behind." [True.] "And we serve in the same sequence." [True.] See, we are serving, just like Neanderthal man served. And he calibrated around 70 or something like that, 70. Cro-Magnon man, Neanderthal man.

So, it's like we're part of an evolution, then, and then by willingness and grace, we accept our role in this evolution of consciousness. So, we don't have to be resentful or angry. Let's say, we serve God, then, by merely being a human being, huh? Let's see if that's so. "We can ask that: resist." [True.] "We serve God merely by living out the life of a human being to the best of our potentiality: resist." [True.] Oh ho! So, there is a lot of guilt, right? "The reason I gave her the finger, God, is I was trying to evolve my consciousness to overcome my fear of being assertive, overcome my Protestant, inhibited background."

When I was a boy, I was very religious, and I was scrupulous. The thought of doing that would just, oh my God, "You can't go to Communion tomorrow morning. The *thought* of putting your finger in the air, but *doing* it, however, would be too horrendous to admit to the priest. Oh, Father, I have sinned, oh my God. I gave a woman the finger and did it in Basha's parking lot." That's at least 50 Hail Marys and a 120 Our Fathers.

Oh wow. We have angelic nature on one side and that animal on the other side. And here, we're balanced, then, between the—so, the evolution of *Homo spiritus*—we are a single documentation of evolution at this point. "So, we are part of the soon-to-erupt *Homo spiritus*: resist." [True.] If we weren't *Homo spiritus*, nobody would be in this room. Yeah. We *are Homo spiritus*. That's a lot different than Cro-Magnon man, a lot different than . . . a lot different than lots of people . . . who are still on the planet, hah! They should get off, shouldn't they? So, on the planet, then, we have a whole mix. From the very bottom, we have some humans that calibrate lower than animals. They always claim they're innocent too. That's one mark of guilt. They always say they're innocent. The DNA is all over, and his fingerprints are everywhere: "I'm innocent."

So, on the planet at this time, then, we have the whole galaxy of evolution, all the way from the most horrendous to the most beatific. All the way to Buddha, Jesus Christ, Krishna; all the great saints; Mother Teresa, Ramana Maharshi, all the names that we revere, because they document where consciousness has evolved, what they represent. What does Mother Teresa represent? She represents unconditional love, the heart at 700.

So, as consciousness evolves into the higher energies of love, a lot of what the ego is involved in, when the ego is dominated from down here (below 200), its content, what you're laying in bed at night thinking about, is totally different than when you put it in the context of lovingness. In lovingness, now, if you're still annoyed with somebody, you try to see it differently, because dislike, hatred, regret, resentments are no longer pleasant; they're painful. They're like a splinter, and when you're angry, you don't mind it, you know, when you're angry. When you're in a lower energy field, that which is nonintegrous doesn't bother you.

As you evolve in consciousness, though, now you can't tolerate the nonintegrous anymore. Your old pirate shipmates are no longer welcome in your life. They try to come back in your life, and you say, "Well, my life has taken a different way, you know what I mean? I just don't feel like going out and killing anymore." "What's happened to the old Dave, man? You lost your spirit, boy!" "Then we're going to hit some waterfront dive and get into a brawl, man, and the broads, and knock a few teeth in, you know." They used to do that, I mean, even in this lifetime. In World War II, you know, I was on a mine sweep. The biggest fun was, you'd hit shore, you'd hit the bars. And they called me "Shorty." In those days people weren't into political correctness; if you're short, they called you "Shorty." Nobody cared about it. We loved each other for that. Even at that point in my life, I just was not into brawling. But you also have to have a macho image, so you can't look like you're a coward. So, how do you get out of brawling? Well, if you're not a very good brawler, they'd say, "Shorty, you stand over there." And then, whap, whap, whap! Whap, whap, whap. That's what they did, you know. Stand out of the way.

Anyway, that's not exactly what you're into, and we've said before, if you take a waterfront dive, you clean it up, new owner puts in new carpets, puts new drapes, puts new lighting in, paints the whole place, makes a nice new sign. He opens up a month later, none of the old crowd goes there anymore. You've changed the energy; you've changed the energy field.

So, as we become more integrous, then, that which is less than integrous we can no longer tolerate. There's a certain field, a certain level of lovingness here, there's a certain level of lovingness here where you can't see anything except innocence and lovingness. You can only see people as being innocent and loving. And you loan your money to crooks. You loan your car to car thieves. Your analyst says you're in denial about the negatives of life, and you think to yourself, "What negative?" You know what I mean? "I don't know what this guy's talking about." You say, "Well, he's probably of a lower consciousness. Oh, he sees negative things in people. Well, God bless him. Dear Lord, please help this man's spirit so he sees the pure innocence of all that exist." Right. Well, you see, you're looking at the Self, but your physicality is in a physicality, in which you can get hit by the bus. So, the error is to mix levels, mix levels. I told you, when I talked about *A Course in Miracles*, "Trust your brother." I have my doubts about that one. It cost me a couple hundred thousand, as a matter of fact. And so, I have a question about that particular lesson. The rest of them I go for.

We become less and less able to tolerate the nonintegrous. Now, sometimes the nonintegrous are relatives or somebody that you have an investment with, et cetera. And now you've got to transcend the attachment to that, you know? Why? Because it's not that the nonintegrous themselves are dangerous to your life; it's very unlikely they will be. I mean, so they take away all your money, you know. In the space I was in, I couldn't care less. You want all the money? Take it. I used to put a bag of money by my front door, and if there's anybody who didn't have money, there's some. Help yourself. So, it wasn't that; it's if something is nonintegrous in your life, what happens is, it's a doorway through which the energies of that which is nonintegrous now have a play with your life. So, it's more that you want to plug up the hole, the leak. It's that they're a leak, and through them come all kinds of things. Your brakes fail, battery goes dead, the ceiling begins to leak. You wonder where the hell is all this coming from.

It's the energy field, then. So, you know, Jesus said to avoid that. Don't oppose it; pray for it. People that are evolved see the innocence behind it. You can see the innocence behind it and still decline it. So, that is the balance. So, it's a matter of balance. It's a matter of the third eye of the Buddhic body, really, to see that that is nonintegrous. At the same time, it is innocent. At the same time, you can't allow it to walk around the house. You can love the cobra for its intrinsic beauty, for that which it is, but you can't really let him run around the house. Why? Because you're going to sit in your chair someday and forget the cobra is there, and goodbye, there you go. My mind is also a comedian. It's always thinking of funny things. And I have to stem that. A cobra bite in the tail is always fatal, you know. In the leg, it's okay, but a cobra bite there, it's goodbye. So, you can't have a cobra in the house because you might sit on it, and uh . . . So, that would be an unwanted result. So, the nonintegrous brings into your life the unwanted result, and it does it innocently by nature of its own energy, of which it is unaware. It isn't that it's hateful, vicious, destructive; it's just that this dog has fleas. I love Rover, but he's got fleas, folks, and when you get fleas in the house—anybody ever get dog fleas in the house? Oh boy, it's something getting them out. One day our cat got into the fleas. Man, it was like six months of fighting fleas. You wouldn't guess how I finally found them. Anyway, the fleas had gotten into the rug of the car. So, the house is sprayed and exterminated, and two weeks later, there's fleas in the house. Where in the hell are they coming from? They're in the rug of the car. See, once it gets in, it's like fleas. The way I found out—anyway, I found the last flea in the house. I found out where he was.

So, in the evolution of our consciousness, we go through, really, I think, quite difficult and trying periods. Even lovingness itself, you see, has a downside. When you see everyone as innocent and loving, one day your car is missing from the parking lot.

Now, at that level, it doesn't really matter. In that state of consciousness, cars come, cars go, big deal. In the physical domain, insurance will pay for it. I mean, it's a nothing, really. It's a nuisance; you've got to rent a car and all that, but you're failing to see the meaning of it: that you allowed that opportunity to be there by allowing something in your life that you really don't need to be there. It isn't that you can't live it through; it isn't that you can't overcome it. Of course you can. Your insurance will pay you. You'll get another car. So, what do you lose? You lose time and energy. You've lost time and energy, and you've been distracted from something that might have been more beneficial to the world and society and yourself.

So, we're talking about sort of subtle things, because people who are seriously committed, you know, have really lots of strange experiences, and I think sharing them with each other is very beneficial. And the books I've written have got extremely wide distribution. We get all kinds of letters and phone calls and e-mails; I mean, it's a torrent of communications. And a lot of them include, you might say, oddities of human behavior. Things you don't read about, you don't see them in the movies, you don't see them on television, but people have subjective, *very* different kinds of experiences. And, you know, in 50 years of psychiatry, I've heard everything, but since I wrote this book and I started getting mail from out in the world there, there's more things I have never even heard about as a psychiatrist, I tell you. Strange dislocations between spirit and body, strange alterations in consciousness. People fall into the so-called *siddhis* for a while. And the miraculous begins to happen all over the place. And they find that consciousness can affect electronic equipment.

And then there's all kinds of strange things, and they don't know what to make of it. I always tell them it's best not to mention this to anybody, frankly. Read up on the siddhis; it's there in the Sanskrit literature, it's classic. But I really wouldn't confide it in other people. And when I went through that period, frankly, I didn't. Of the few times I did, I wished I hadn't. And uh, besides, people—the ordinary people that are around you won't even see what you're seeing anyway. So—because you're living on a different level, vibrational level of consciousness, you might say, and they are not even witnessing what you witness. And the lady gets up and walks away without her cane. You say, "You see that?" They say, "Well, she didn't have a cane before, there wasn't a cane sitting there." So, what can you say about such things? Nothing.

A lot of these phenomena—so, that's one positive reason for becoming associated with other people who are spiritually committed, hmm? In the old days, classically, we left the world, we joined our spiritual community, and such things were well-known, documented; they've been known for centuries. Now we tend to be more isolated from each other. We meditate by ourselves; although we attend meetings, and all, there isn't that constant interchange of communication. So, we need each other's support in ways that are not so easily obtained in today's world. Although I think, you know, the Internet, which I don't understand it all, but there are, like, websites where people talk to each other about these things, so there is that need for communication, these phenomena in your life. Many things are not comprehensible until they're recontextualized, huh?

So, when we say, where are we in the evolution of consciousness? And we pick out where we are, and we see that we're a part of an evolving species, and probably in 10 million years or less than that, we're going to be replaced by something. For one thing, they'll have to have a better nervous system, because this human nervous system is only scheduled to go up to 600. At 600, the state is one of bliss, as you go up into higher and higher lovingness. These states here, you can't stop crying; everything—two people look at each other, a mother looks at her child, and instantly you break out in tears. It's just, you can't—or music. I've got some music. We hear this tape we play, and at the end of the one that Brock brought back, at the end of that tape, put some beautiful music which I can't handle. Because as soon as that music starts, I wouldn't be able to lecture. You instantly break out into tears because the beauty and the incredible sense of the Presence becomes overwhelming, and it wipes out all functioning in the world. And therefore, spiritual communities serve a very, very valuable service, because within that community, it's safe to share. I'm talking about a legitimate spiritual community, not some of that sort-of-bizarre—you can't mention those that occur along the roadside someplace—but those which, if you calibrate them, are integrous. That state of lovingness, then, becomes the new context . . . in which that lovingness then becomes the context in which content now takes on a different coloration. So, you could look at context almost like colored lights of different intensity which surround that which you're looking at, and how those lights are focused, and their intensity totally changes how you see it, because it's a holographic universe and what you see is the product of the position from which you're seeing it. Which is why quantum mechanics offers us the intellect that rose from the logical Newtonian paradigm of reality to the more powerful spiritual reality.

From the pathway of negation, we might end up at the Void and say, "There's nobody here, there's nobody to answer, and therefore, there's no questions."

DON'T MIX LEVELS

As we evolve spiritually, we're constantly presented with ambiguities. One way to see your way out of an ambiguity is to ask if you're mixing levels. Are you mixing levels? Things are true within a certain context. In another context, they're no longer valid, you understand? Jesus said, "Render unto Caesar that which is Caesar's, and to God, that which is God's." So, in other words, don't mix the levels. Don't think you can walk around without paying your taxes, because they'll put you away. Of course, prison's a good place to meditate, and you can become enlightened in jail. And some people pull that one on themselves, you know. People over the centuries have gotten enlightened in prison. And, uh, "I can't get away from this world, God." Bang! You've just been arrested, you've got 10 years in solitary, you got it! Monastery for one. I told you how I lived in a monastery for one. And the body disappeared, I walked into a wall;

when I walked past a mirror, there was somebody in the house. I'll invite them in. There's somebody in the house, for Christ's sake. "Who is that?" Oh my God, it's myself! What a surprise!

* * *

We have found that kinesiology is a technique available to people who themselves are integrous. Integrity means calibrate at 200 or over. There's an enormous amount of power given to you. To be able to use kinesiology to find out things is an enormous jump in power, and that power is just not given to people who would misuse it. So, one reason that I delayed publishing *Power vs. Force* is, I worried about that. I thought, everybody is going to be using it to build better atomic bombs and kill each other better, you know? So, I worried about it, and anyway, it later came to me that it could only be used by integrous people for integrous ends. So, the intention of the question itself has to be integrous. And you can change a nonintegrous question into an integrous one if you recontextualize it from a different context. And the classic one is: say, "In the interest of the good of all of life." You know, "In the interest in the goodness of all of life for everyone, I have permission to ask this question." So, then you ask, "I have permission to ask this question?" And even though we've done it hundreds of thousands of times, as you've seen during some of these classes, we're beginning to get a *no*. And we don't have time to check out the reason for the *no* at the moment. But it's something you put aside, and you say, "That's something I'll have to investigate later."

So, because 85 percent of the population is below 200—when I wrote *Power vs. Force*, I was naive about that. I thought, "Wow, everybody can do kinesiology." Then I found out later, no, you can only do it if you're over 200. Then I looked at the calibrated scale of consciousness, and I realized that only—that means 15 percent of the population can do it. Of that 15 percent . . . is it 10 percent that has something wrong with their chi energy? Let's ask: "Right now, approximately 15 percent of the population can use it." [True.] "Of that 15 percent, 10 percent have some problem with their chi energy. That is correct." [True.] Yeah, even people who are integrous. Not everybody is adept at it, so it's only *one* way of ascertaining truth. Don't forget, kinesiology is really—you know, it's really a research technique. You don't *need* it to reach enlightenment. The Buddha didn't know kinesiology, and all the great saints that ever lived—Mother Teresa never heard of it, see. And at the time I corresponded with Mother Teresa, Jesus Christ was under attack, I think the front cover of *Time*: "Jesus Christ, did he ever really live? Was he a schizophrenic, homosexual," you know what I mean? All this kind of stuff that periodically surfaces. And so, the reality of the Divinity of Jesus Christ was under attack, you know. Those things come up periodically. So, I just thought Mother Teresa would be interested in that there's a scientific way of validating the Divinity of Christ, as part of the armamentarium of the knowingness of the religious community. So, anyway, it's really a research tool. Occasionally it would be very useful in your life, but's it's not as useful as you may think it is, because understanding comes out of the advancement of one's own consciousness. We use it very often because we're answering questions from other people or because we're investigating new areas. You know, in the writings we do and the videotapes, and all. We're looking into things that mankind has never had access to, never had access to. It's like X-rays or the electron microscope. There are whole areas of life that there was no way of investigating, and now we have ways of investigating it, and of course, we're always coming up with questions ourselves. The answer to one question, you know, leads to the next, and there is, of course, that technique of self-testing, which some people are also good at. So, that's all I can say about kinesiology, it's a thing in itself.

Now we have some specific questions about illnesses. Illnesses seem to be karmic consequences. They take a very specific form; they have a very specific duration. Most illnesses are cyclic in nature. If the illness did not exist before and you have it now, it's obviously not permanent; so, if it cycled in, it can also cycle out. What I tell patients in the office, no matter what ails you, if it cycled into your life, it can also cycle out. As you evolve in consciousness, it doesn't matter whether it cycles in or out; it doesn't matter anymore. People do the *Course in Miracles* in order to recover from certain illnesses, and I tell them, if you're successful with *A Course in Miracles*, you won't care whether the illness leaves or not, because you transcend it, and you know, you learn how to live with various physical things. Because you don't focus on them, they're irrelevant. I've got, you know, right now, two or three things that if I think about it, oh yes, and uh, I had to do an exercise to get off the rug this morning, because my back went out from shoveling the other day—various trivia like that, but it's all trivia. And I'm sure everything like that serves multiple purposes. I like the lesson in the *Course in Miracles* that says you're only subject to what you hold in mind. It doesn't mean you're going to be able to discover consciously what you're holding in mind and from what lifetime, but it is an avenue of approaching which offers some hope of relief. And in my own life, it really worked quite well.

UNDERSTANDING MUSCLE TESTING

[Q]: "When you do kinesiology, are you looking without, within, or what?"

I'm not looking anywhere. So, I'll just explain kinesiology one last time. The next person who asks about it is going to really get it! "What I'm holding in mind is true: resist." [True.] Thank you. She did not *hear* what I'm holding in mind. So, that answers the question. It isn't what the test subject believes that's going to influence your answer. The answer is, no, I didn't tell her what it is. Those are questions that first come up when you first learn kinesiology. The first class I ever went to, that came up, of course. And it's been looked at and answered by thousands and thousands of practitioners over many years. And the answer's always the same; no, it's the reaction of consciousness itself to the presence of truth. And a *no* answer is not a no; it's that truth is not present. So, it's not yes versus no; it's yes versus not-yes. Otherwise, we get into the polarity of the opposites. Truth is either present or it is not present. The electricity is either on or not on. There is no condition of electricity called "off-ness." So, we're not testing "on-ness" versus "off-ness." "On-ness" is either present or not present. The light bulb goes on. So, is that clear? I always begin with the dualities of, you know, good versus bad, and all the rest of that.

[Q]: *"How can our actions bring about changes in the world if it's not via the mechanism of cause? How do actions have consequences?"*

We see that actions—that one action has followed another, so, from a strictly scientific viewpoint, we could say they were sequential. Sequential to what? Sequential to observation. You can't say in-and-of-themselves "sequential," because that's just a concept that you're projecting. If certain conditions prevail, then we have noticed throughout time a certain sequence of perceptions. From a strictly ultrascientific viewpoint, that's all you can say about it. To be strictly truthful, all you can ever say is "what you observe," "what appears to be," because to know that something is happening there, the only way you'd know it is, you'd have to *be* it. You'd have to *be* it. That is a subtle point, of course. And the jump into quantum mechanics is, there's observables, and our language is catching up, and I'm very pleased with it: the word *perceived*—*perceived* is now entering our language. I "perceived" this; I "perceived" that. That leaves room for the subjectivity, so it's closer to reality. The perceived event, the perceived witness, perceived event. That means you've introduced back—into a person-less, dead world—subjectivity. Because it is only subjectivity that has any reality to it. Observables all depend on the observer and the point of observation and the definitions and symbols, and it is far removed from the actuality itself. So, when we say, "perceived event," that is certainly closer to reality.

THE IMPORTANCE OF CHOICE

It's choice, it's choice to let that which is nonintegrous go from one's life. In many peoples' spiritual evolution, this is a crucial area. And we see many people in a town like Sedona, for instance, who leave everything and everyone, and all their titles and buildings and money and relationships and everything, and give up everything for God, and then drive a bus to make ends meet, you know. So, we see the willingness to sacrifice everything for God. If that everything, if whatever it is, is nonintegrous, it *has* to go, sooner or later. It has to go. And it's sort of a test. The willingness to surrender everything to God, to step over one's own children and every little—you walk away from that which is nonintegrous. One may have to walk away from one's own child and surrender that to God. "Well, God, he's your problem now." You go to Al Anon and learn that one. That's his problem, and I'm going to live my life.

It isn't that you plug the leak. You make a choice, and you don't do it out of a make-wrong. See, because at the same time, you're seeing innocence. The reason we're talking about this is because spiritual people, as they evolve, they have big areas of naivete. The devotee, the initiate is a long way from the spiritual master. A lot of gray hairs to go through before you go from initiate to master. So, there is a period of naivete, and it comes when you see the innocence and lovability of all things. When you get into the lovingness, you can only see the innocence and lovableness and beauty of all that exists. And you think the guy who just stole your car is great. "He looked just like my dad," you know what I mean? Sweet old man. And he just walked off with the keys to your car. Uh huh. So, there is that gap. And so, what you see is, you see the innocence of all beings, which you really need to see to transcend to an enlightened state. Intrinsically, all that lives is . . . its own nature is innocent. It does what it's programmed to do. Some of the behaviors are programmed by evolution itself, by the very function of the brain itself. The lion chases its lunch and eats it; it doesn't kill anything, understand? It's innocent in what it does. It's just being a lion. If you're a lion, rabbits look yummy. And we started out the last lecture—that lady that had the lifetime lion, and they wrote a book about her and a movie, and all. In the end, the lion ate her because he loved her. We checked that out, right? He didn't kill her because he hated her. He loved her so much, he—"I could just eat you up"—and he did. Enjoyed every bite, oh man! All right. So, even though you love the lion and you see its intrinsic innocence, it can eat you. And in the end, if you're not aware, it can eat you. So, I see these trainers, you know, put their head in the mouth of an alligator for the camera, and they put their head in the mouth of the lion, and you know it's only a matter of time before his head's going to get eaten off. I know the alligator is going to bite his head off one day. I just know it. Why? Because an alligator is an alligator. Don't you get it?

So, all right, so, this idea of safety: let's say, we see the innate innocence of all that is, including people that are overcome by insanity. Religious insanity—one of the forms of insanity is religious mania, and it can become almost epidemic. We saw it in Europe. Religious mania became epidemic. Now we see it in the Middle East. The religious delusions become almost epidemic, you know. They all begin to believe in that. And Europe went through that with Christianity and various perversions of Christianity.

So, the person whose mind is taken over by delusional thinking, the reason his mind is taken over by delusional thinking is because it has no way of protecting itself. It doesn't know truth from falsehood. You watch on the TV channel how the German children were trained in the 1930s. It was fantastic. I wish I was there, you know. I watched it. I said, "Wow, what a childhood!" They all like go to camp, and they hang around the campfire and they sing "Deutschland über alles" and "Heil to the Führer, who's our savior." It's a fantastic life. I mean, it was a great life, just was like being in the Boy Scouts around the clock, you know what I mean? Whatever you do, you are serving your country and the pride. The fact the leader was not integrous, how would they know that? How would they know that? They were only children. So, how can you blame them? So, you see the innocence of all that lives, *and* you have to tie up your camel. Does anybody know that quote? "I believe in God, but I tie up my own camel." Yeah, there it is, okay. All right, that's a good lesson. We tie up our own camel because we don't want to mix levels. We don't want to mix levels. And, although the person is basically innocent, and probably taken over by some lower-astral, possessing spirit . . . I'm thinking of a killer right now: "We have permission to ask: resist." [True.] "He's taken over by a lower astral: resist." [True.] Okay. All right.

Almost all the famous killers that you read about, they are usually given nicknames—you know, "Killer John," or something like that. And he's killed 20 or 30 by now, by the time they catch him. And uh, anyway, what about his innocence? Was there some part of him that said yes to him? To that entity? Well, there's some vulnerability. He left a hole open there somewhere, right where that entity came in and took over his consciousness. How do we know that? Because very often on TV, you'll hear him say, "I didn't do it. It wasn't me that did it." You hear him say, "It wasn't me. It wasn't me that did it." I believe they're right: "It wasn't me." It was some other aspect from some other realm, but he left that porthole open for it to come in. Very often, it's drugs. Very often, it's some crime. Sometimes there's something innocent, like brain injury. So, there's many karmic reasons why the porthole was left open for the entity to get in. As we become more responsible, then there's a point at which we really do have to go through our spiritual library and take out the energy of that which is nonintegrous. All the "end of the world" books, and "the world's ending in 19 so and so." I've lived through so many "ends of the world." I mean, I know in Sedona, there's a new end of the world every lecture series, you know. They got it from some entity on the other side in the year 19 so and so. I've been through 20 of them already in Sedona. California was falling off into the ocean; earthquakes were happening; the vortexes were going to explode, and spaceships were going in and out. I mean, there's no end to that bullshit. But it brings 'em in, I'll tell you, brings 'em in. "Let's go out, baby, and watch the spaceships tonight. See those lights in the sky? They're speaking to me," and, uh. . . . You're supposed to eat nothing but radishes, live in the desert, and wait for them to come and get you. They've already got you, folks, I hate to tell you. How have they got you? They want you to be in their power with this mystification. So, that which has a circuslike atmosphere, that which sounds far-out and bizarre, do you know what? If it sounds nonsensical, ah, all right.

So, to be on guard, then, is something that leads from spiritual naivete. The spiritually naive are drawn to places like Sedona, where the astral circus is a continuous, round-the-clock seven days a week. There's a psychic reading on every street corner. They want to read your runes, read your stones, read your knobs, read your physiognomy, read your toes, you know what I mean? Got a new breathing technique: breathe six times, count to seven three times—I've told you about how I used to stop, when I was hitchhiking. I'd go seven, seven, seven, seven, and I'd turn around seven times, and the truck would stop and pick me up hitchhiking. All right. Seven times seven, that would stop the truck. I was living out in the country, you know, and it was 10 below zero, and I would hear—there was a car every 10 minutes, so a truck, when I could hear it, it was exciting, you know. I'd wave out there, hitchhiking, you know. Then I'd hear him hit the air brakes, whoosh, and as soon I heard those air brakes, I knew I had a ride, you know, it was great.

What we know about the kinesiologic test, then, is that it's limited to certain people, probably for certain reasons, you know. There are many other ways to find out the truth. You begin to realize that the truth is that which brings you love and happiness, and anything else is fallacious. There's probably some other way we're going to be able to substitute for people who are not themselves adept at it.

[Q]: "How do you handle people that are in your life that are nonintegrous?"

Well, Jesus said to avoid them. You join any serious spiritual order, they're going to tell you you're going to have to leave them. What if you have to work with them? If you have to work with them, then you are coming from a certain specific role, a certain archetype; you're coming from the healer. That's different than having an affair with them; you're not supposed to have affairs with patients. Let's see: "The healer is protected by the archetype, by the role of the healer, from being damaged by the patient: resist." [True.] I myself have stopped taking patients of a certain calibrated level, and in fact we test them out with kinesiology before I even call them back. And, uh, it's an unwillingness on my part anymore to deal with what I dealt with for so many years. That's just a personal choice. But that's exactly what we do; we check them out. So-and-so wants an appointment; I check him out. "No." Okay. I don't ask why. I just assume that God's will for me is that this is not the kind of person I should probably spend time with.

These various states of consciousness *are* their own reality. They *are* their own reality, on an experiential basis. The experience of hell is extremely hellish. These are all different levels of consciousness. Each one is valid within its own domain. Each one is valid within itself.

The teachings of all the great teachers—you know, what Jesus taught was, avoid anything that calibrates below 200. That's all he said, right? That's all he said. And traditionally it's called "sin," but it is really just everything under 200. Greed, avarice, malice, hatred, all these things, he said avoid all that, because if you hang out in it, when you leave the body, you will go to the realm that calibrates at that level. You will go to the realm like a cork in water, is the way I say it. You don't have to worry about what happens to your soul when it leaves the body, because it's like a cork in water, and because of the absolute justice of all of creation, it will automatically gravitate to that to which it is aligned. It'll automatically gravitate to that with which it is aligned. There is nothing arbitrary going on in the universe. There is nothing arbitrary. The justice of God is absolute, infinite, and impeccable. Each thing only experiences out of its own spiritual decisions that which it has chosen. Having experienced that, it may change its mind. Haha, and how! In the pit of hell, I said, "If there is a God, I ask him for help." That was when the last possible anything-ness was removed. When you see that hell goes on for eternity—*for-ev-er*—without any possibility under any circumstance of escaping from it, bam, there goes your last card up your sleeve. Then it took that before you said, "If there is a God, I ask him to help me." Shewww! And then to the opposite end of the spectrum.

So, each is its reality on its own level. The spectacular Presence, the infinite realization: it's like God presents its Divinity to you. It isn't that you seek it; it shines forth and stares at you, and like a shock you realize it, you realize what it is you're looking at. So, each thing is what it is, on its own level.

Say that is an illusion—see, the question is, "Is there a hell, or is it only an illusion of the ego?" Any condition can be defined, you see; there's different points of view. Experientially it was as real or more real than anything that I'd ever experienced in my life. Hopeless, endless agony that went on for eons. That certainly would knock out any questions about whether there is a hell. I guess that answered *that* question, didn't it? Boy! So, we don't want to challenge hell, folks; it's just not a good thing.

These inner states, there are not many people in the world that will understand them, and that's the value of a spiritual community as well. Other people have had these states, and they know what it is, where you can't stop crying for a couple of years, you know. Everything you look at, there's certain music; you would not be able to function and listen to that music. There's one—Brock put a piece of music at the end of this "Om Namaha Shivaya" tape, and if I'm going to function, I have to get out of the room, because its beauty is just paralyzing. You just can't move. So, you have to get used to these states, learn how to function. The next lecture I'm going to have to learn, how do you talk about that which paralyzes you with exquisite bliss? How do you talk about it at the same time you're experiencing it? I don't know. I'll find out next time. So, most humans, then, there's no limit to the level of which your consciousness can leap. There are certainly karmic influences. The most intense thing is the willingness to surrender to God at extreme depths. Extreme depths. And perhaps what was shocking in the evolution of this consciousness was the degree of the depths to which it had to go. It was beyond all imagination to have to go to that depth to let go of whatever that blockage was. I never went back and checked out with kinesiology what was the blockage that made it so necessary to go to such a great depth, you know. Hitting bottom, how deep does the bottom have to be? I mean . . . and yet we see it every day, people who've lost everything they've had; I see people at a counseling center. He's been five times in prison now. His wife has left him, his children have left him, his health is gone, he's got all kinds of charges hanging over him, and he sits there and he says, "I don't have a problem with alcohol." And you go, "What does it take, man? What does it take?" You know? Do you have to chop off each finger one by one, and get to toe number eight before he says, "Yeah, I've got a problem with alcohol"? What is it going to take? I don't know.

The Unmanifest has within it the quality, the potentiality of becoming manifest. Now, the question really is, what moves Divinity from the Unmanifest to the manifest? I don't know. Amusement, maybe. Nothing more comical than the human race, huh? "I think I'm bored. I think I'll make mankind and sit back. It's like watching the Animal Channel, huh?"

[Q]: "Can a person go down in consciousness?"

Yes, unfortunately. People can—It happens to spiritual teachers very often. Very often, you see, they write a book up here, in the high 500s, and then you check them out years later and you find that they calibrate at 1—what do they usually calibrate? Down here someplace. So, that which begins to have an impact and dispel negativity begins to, you might say, a power struggle between—for dominion over man. If a person's evolution of their consciousness gets high enough, it begins to threaten the dominance of negativity, which then fights back and says, "Having sex with your devotees is a way of blessing them and sharing God's exquisite Presence as love." Next thing you know, the guru's on the Internet. He's having sex with this person and that person. "Wealth is an expression of God's abundance: accumulate the millions." Do you know what I mean? They fall, and we've already expressed that . . . in previous things.

Each one, when you sort of get to a certain level, it's like the test of its opposite comes up. It's like the test . . . fame, fortune, power over others, glamour, falling for your own publicity; those are all the dangers. So, there could be a chink in the armor. You see, that's where something nonintegrous allowed some entity or energy to come in, and nobody except people who are like students in these classes, to my knowledge, are sufficiently warned in advance of what's going to come up and how it's going to come up, and how to look at it, and what's out about it. What's out about it is that the context is out about it. Content only: the Luciferic is very, very, very clever. It can present something so convincingly that you're sure that Jesus himself would agree with it. Some knowingness somewhere warns you, and then, as you refuse the temptation, the context—shewww!—shines forth, and you see what the error was. The error is one of context.

I remember in this lifetime the Luciferic coming up, and it was the same Luciferic sentence that I'd seen other gurus—and in fact, some of them I'd met—they fell for the exact phrase. I recognized the phrase, and I know what phrase it was and how it came up: "Now that you're beyond personal karma and there is no wrathful God to answer for, all power is yours. Own it." And that's where they fall. I was all by myself. It's like you're all alone on a . . . I don't know what level of consciousness that comes in at, but it's sort of routine when it comes in. And the error there is, you may be beyond personal karma, but you are not beyond the karma of the Presence of God as the totality of the universe. You may be beyond your personal crap from previous lifetimes, but you sure are not beyond the infinite justice of God, which is infinite. But the temptation is, now that you have transcended personal karma—which at that point, you have—that you're subject to being a consciousness within the domain of the reality of the infinity of the Allness of God himself, so. And besides, these temptations come up, and what do they want to give you? Power. I came up with, "What do I want power for? Power for what?" "All power is yours. Own it." All you're doing is validating your own Divinity. Very convincing. If you can manifest abundantly, have 90 Mercedes-Benzes, or whatever—very appealing. If you're beyond sin, why not have sex with dozens? Hmm, right? All right. So, it comes on in a very convincing way, except that the context, the context is fallacious. The error is one of context.

So, the spiritually naive person is evolved as far as content, but their understanding of context hasn't expanded enough to fortify them against that temptation. What would you want power for? I mean, it's a drag. It's like money. The more you own, the more horrible it is, you know what I'm saying? You've got a bad life with one car—it's going to get worse with two. Get up to four—right now we have four or five, I think. It's horrible. It's horrible, really awful. We've got all these dependents—it's like a bunch of dependents that you've got to take care of, you know? Everything you own now becomes like a chain that owns you, you know what I mean? So, why would you want power and wealth and all those things? All right. But that is a convincing kind.

So, as we go up, we're tempted by chinks in our armor. We have to become really quite erudite and quite sophisticated to survive spiritually. As you get up to lovingness, the challenges are going to come up, you know. Challenges are going to come up. And finally you come up to a point where you say, "I love you, I love you, and you must leave by tomorrow, or I'll call the sheriff." It isn't that I don't love the person that's the problem. The problem is that I love the person. And that is the problem. The problem is that I see the innate innocence. The person doesn't know better. Can a psychopath help being a psychopath? I don't think so. I think there's something in the pre—current science that shows there that the frontal lobe, frontal cortex, is deficient in the psychopath. It shows up at age one and a half, age three: no capacity to delay gratification and impulsivity, and all these things.

Now, getting rid of that which you love, that's what's hard, see. That, because it's now required, it's an exercise you learn how to do. You let go of your attachment to that person, that relative, that car, that spouse, whatever it is. You're not going to reach a great deal of enlightenment if this person keeps pulling you back into this energy field over and over and over again.

The demand becomes different as you progress spiritually. You're progressing from spiritual naivete that stops at every street corner for a psychic reading, and you go through naivete, and then, through often painful experiences, you develop spiritual maturity. You don't become spiritual—you don't own your own spiritual mastery from the level of naivete. You know?

[Q]: "Does the U.S. have the right to determine outcomes of conflicts in other countries? And what would God say?"

Well, I asked Him the other day, in fact, just this very question. To me, that situation is people working their way out of the 70s. We're talking about people caught in the spleen, see. So, it's like an astral dimension that's manifesting on this physical universe. Nobody there's interested in peace. In fact, the biggest enemies they have are peace. If you get out there and shout about peace, they assassinate you, you're a threat to everything. Haha! Their whole lifestyle's under threat. What would they want peace for? You know, in a prizefight, you want somebody to come up and say, "Stop hitting each other"? I mean, the prizefight, that's what it's about, isn't it? Because these are people that are evolving. The calibrated level of the consciousness of that conflict—let's just do it and then be done with this subject: "We have permission to do that conflict: resist." [True.] "It's over 70." [True.] "It's over 80." [Not true.] It's around about the level of the reptile: 70. Savage hatred, evil, the spleen. So, they're living out the world of the spleen. So, you don't transcend the spleen until you evolve past the spleen, so I suppose there is some lifetime in which you've got to be very splenic. You've got to learn how to hate, learn how to kill. So, I just wouldn't vacation there. I think in the book, we said the Holy Lands calibrate about 90, and everybody wants to—is totally interested in—but the Holy Lands are about 90. The Empire State Building calibrates at 425, so if you want to go to a holy place to meditate, the 102nd floor, for some reason, calibrates higher than the 86th floor. The 86th floor of the Empire State Building is where most people get off. And the little, tiny elevator—if you want, you can go up to 102. For some reason that calibrates about 20 points higher. I don't know why, but it does. Less idiots, less cowards up there. Who knows what it is. I don't know.

[Q]: "So, what are the best ways to heal shame?"

Shame: somebody asked me that, because that is a tough one until you recontextualize it. Shame is really vanity, pride. Shame is pride projected onto society and visited back upon yourself. You let go of the pridefulness and own that being a human leaves you to be fallible. It's okay to be stupid and make terrible mistakes. It's inevitable. How can you evolve unless you make really bad mistakes, huh? You can't—so, shame is then looking at your own behavior from the viewpoint of pride, see. From pride, this looks like disgraceful behavior, but if you let go of pride, it looks more like stupidity is innate to the human condition. Ignorance is what we're all born here with. We have a hardware computer with no programs on it, right, when we are born here. So, we're obviously—shame is a technique used by parents, see. It's a misfortunate one. "Shame on you!" You know. To teach the child to shame oneself is sort of a—not too great a technique. It's good for my business, though. I prescribe Prozac, and all this stuff really helps, helps with shame. So, they build up my business, but it's not really a very good technique, because what happens is, we make mistakes out of ignorance. And why are we ignorant? Because we're born with a tabula rasa, we're born with the hardware of a computer and no programming. So, we're now at the effect, we're victims of our own programming. That's how you can have compassion for all of mankind. You see that everyone was once a happy little baby, who got programmed by all this. So, he is now the victim of his own ego. He's the victim of his own fallacious belief systems. He's a victim. . . . We don't feel sorry for him. We don't make excuses for him. And we avoid him. But we also see that, despite that degree of negativity, the innate innocence is still there; otherwise you couldn't program him. You couldn't train all those little children in Germany to become good Nazis unless they were innocent and trusting to begin with. It was their innocence and trust. What comes to my mind about that kind of thing, though, is Jesus Christ said, "Woe to those who rape the innocence of children. Woe to those who abuse the innocence of children, for their fate is pretty grim."

So, don't the religious zealots who program the innocence of children to believe such negativity . . . It seems to me, it's rather karmically horrific. It would scare the wits out of me. Scare the wits out of me to tell somebody to kill somebody else for God, you know. I mean, what if you were wrong, you know what I mean? Even with kinesiology I wouldn't believe it, you know. The karmic consequence of raping the innocence of the consciousness of the naive is the negative karma, then, and . . . why we have to avoid that which is not integrous. The false guru—it scares me in the name of God to teach people to do that which is nonintegrous and rationalize it with some high-sounding thing . . . is not too good.

[Q]: "The good of dreams: What is the dream state?"
I'm not an expert on dreams. I've never trusted dreams. I once, when I was in psychoanalytic training, wrote a refutation; I refuted Freud's theory of dreams, you know. I thought—to me, dreams are an automatic consequence of the brain clearing itself at the end of the day. However, its value in psychoanalysis is that it acts like a Rorschach card. In other words, even if your dream was created by a mechanical dream generator, and now we hypnotize you and say that was your dream, and say, "What does a giraffe remind you of?" we'd get a lot of very valuable information out of it, because now your dream serves like a Rorschach card. So, your associations, what you see there, are the projections from your own unconscious. Let's ask about dreams: "We have permission to ask about dreams: resist." [True.] "In front of this audience now: resist." [True.] "Dreams are the clearing-ness of the apparatus of the brain: resist." [True.] That's what it is, see. Of course, it picks up whatever is lying around to clear it up. It's sort of like there's something in the electronic world, I forget what it is, that when we turn it off, it has to clear itself. It's like, to me, the clearing-ness, clearing-ness. That it's not—let's see: "And yet, within it, we could pick up the prophetic: resist." [True.] "And we do pick up the prophetic." [True.] Yes.

So, if I come back another lifetime, I'll spend that one on dreams and the meaning of dreams and how they tie in with the various levels of consciousness and karmic propensity and the levels of consciousness and symbolism, and that would make a whole Ph.D., you know, a work. So, it's really quite an interesting thing. And I vacillated about the meaning and value of dreams throughout my professional lifetime. And in psychoanalysis, of course, we use them quite extensively, and the resolution of my own psychoanalysis was accomplished via a dream, very literally.

So, I think I told you that dream. It was a famous dream. In fact, it got published in the national psychoanalytical journals. And I always say, if you don't believe in the Oedipal complex, try lying on an analyst's couch one hour a day, five days a week, for a couple of years and see what comes up. Yeah, right. Freud didn't make it up. It's what came out of the unconscious, you know. I can remember a terrifying dream. I was in about the second or third year of psychoanalysis. I saw him every day of the week, laid on the couch, and free-associated, and anyway, I got worse and worse. I got phobic. I couldn't drive over the bridges; I couldn't go under the tunnel. I was afraid of crowds. I was afraid of being alone. I had claustrophobia, agoraphobia, and my analyst was very pleased. Terrific progress! I say, "I'm getting worse." He says, "You're doing terrific." And then the worst of all nightmares. I lay on the analyst's couch and then—telling him this nightmare. And in the nightmare, this lion is killing me. There's some woman off vaguely in the background, and the lion is attacking and killing me. And I jump off the couch, you know. My heart is pounding like that. He says, "What do you think it might have been?" I said, "I don't know, my mind's blank." He says, "What about the lion?" I said, "I don't know. A lion? I don't know." He says, "What's my name?" I said, "Your name's Lionel Ovesey. Oh, *lion*. Oh my God." The unconscious terror of the analyst, the father figure killing me for desiring or fantasying the woman in his life. I'd never met her. You don't believe in the Oedipal complex, I've got news for you. That's how you get gray hair as an analyst. So, dreams in my own experience, then, were very profoundly beneficial. On the other hand, I have a certain doubt about them.

Well, now, to overcome the effects of negativity in your life requires spiritual work, and what you do is, you utilize every technique and thing that you know. You know, you can smudge the room; that's classic. Let's see if that's useful: "Smudging the room with sage is useful." [True.] "It does repel negative energies: resist." [True.] All right, so we start with the most primitive: just smudge the room, that gets the energies out. You pray, you use prayer, use all the things, you ask for a miracle. The consequences, of course, also fulfill certain needs within yourself. There's a need to come out of spiritual naivete into spiritual wisdom. The only way you can do that is, if enough people steal your shoes, you finally get, you can't trust every monk with your shoes. Eventually, a monk's going to steal your shoes. That's right. And you go, "Oh, I have to learn discernment." So, everything that happens in your life has its upside. Its *seeming* downside is the annoyance, the pain, and the seeming loss. But don't forget that every loss is a gain. Don't forget that every grief, every loss is a gain. Where there was a something, there is now freedom.

With total freedom, you lose everything. By the time you reach enlightenment, you've let go of everything, even your own existence, even your own physicality. The dominion of the core of the ego as the sense of "I," as you walk toward *that* gate, you know you're dying. You actually die; you literally, actually experience die-ing. And you realize it is the first time you have ever died, and you are actually facing certain death. The certainty of this death is absolutely certain, and beyond it you have only the trust in the spiritual Presence innate within your own consciousness, heard from some teacher at some time to "walk straight through no matter what." And so that faith takes you through the terror, because at the last moment, it was, in this experience, ter-ror, because it was death itself, and you realize you'd never died before. Every time you left the body, it was like, terrific, and this is real death, so there has to be a willingness to surrender everything all the way down to the absolute bottom.

CHAPTER 5

The Source of Our Existence Is Silence

The substrate of the existence of all this at this moment is silent. The Source of our existence is silent. The rug is silent. This is silent. Everything about us. Do you get what I'm saying? Out of that innate silence, then, is where, as you expand context, you begin to own the silence as yourself and that which is interfering with the silence is the not-self. The sound becomes the content. It's only because of the silence that you can hear any sound. You begin to identify with the silence as that which you are. It comes on profoundly. The oneness with the silence is one's own existence beyond all time. That which I am existed prior to this universe and will be here long after this universe expires, because universes come and go, like the dreams of Indra. The illusion of it all comes and goes. And creating and unfolding universes is how I enjoy myself. That's my prerogative, all right? That's a prerogative. I choose to do that. When you choose it, you're not at the effect of it. So, you choose to experience this existence as you experience it. And in so doing, you let go resisting it, and as you let go resisting it, you dissolve it. And you go back into that which you are prior to this existence, hmm. And that is the meaning of the silence. To be that which you are now, you have to be the whole universe, because it's all part of the whole picture. So, Indra's dream: on the in-breath, a creation arises; on an out-breath, a creation—no, it's the other way—on an out-breath, a creation arises, and on an in-breath, it disappears. Over the millennia. Millennia. You have done it for millennia. All it is, is remembering who you are. That's your Oneness with the Creator.

[Q]: "Now, what is the best way to influence events in the world favorably?"

Well, first of all, you could ask yourself why you want to change events in the world. Then you have to realize that what you mean is your perception of events in the world. The way you see it, you're making certain presumptions, and because of the way you see it in your presumptions, you want to do something about it. So, all those steps are subjects for spiritual—to transcend. The world that you see is not a world of reality; it's a world of perception: yours and other people's. It's the acting out of a melodrama. And everyone, if you check out your prior lives, will find that you were involved in similar things and for the same reasons that people are involved in them now. So, you might say, on the planet there are people that go, "Well, where is our distribution-of-consciousness thing?" On the planet there are people that go from near enlightenment or enlightenment all the way down to the bottom of the pile—what we look at as the bottom of the pile. We look at them as the bottom of the pile, but that's from our point of observation. That's from our point of observation. When we get a person out of apathy, up to angriness, they're making good progress.

But if you see the distribution of the level of consciousness on the planet, you realize that the majority of people are somewhere down the line, farther back on the road, however you want to picture it, you understand? And what do you suppose they are supposed to be doing all day to keep busy? What are all these people going to be doing, you know? Let's see. That the people in this room are way over on the right-hand side there. What about the rest of the people? Have a heart, you know? They need somebody to kill and hate, and all that. I mean, where would you be without an enemy . . . in the Middle East? Nobody to bomb, I mean, it'd be horrible. Your life would lose meaning.

How do you evolve in consciousness? You have to go through the levels. You have to go through the levels. People give up a level when they hit bottom, when this is not the way you want to live, when this is not—when it finally gets you. I was going to make some signs for today. One's called "Palestine," the other one's called "Israel." And in the middle is "attacks and gets even with." And they just switch the cards, hour by hour, you know. Yesterday was this. Every day you just change these two cards, because the news doesn't change. "Hates and gets even with," and you just change. Palestine does it to Israel; Israel does it to Palestine. You just go back and forth like this.

One day, somebody says, "You know, this is stupid." "Hey, this is not getting us anywhere." And that's how you give it up. People give up drinking that way. People give up bad lives, bad marriages, bad lifestyles.

* * *

That's the nature of the evolution of consciousness. The world population can't get to here, high on the Map. It starts out low and comes out of the ooze and evolved up to hominid. We don't see the first hominids until about here, the ape and the monkeys, and we work our way on up. And it's not a precise kind of an evolution. We said the heart, the purr of the kitty is at 500. The kitty's purr is 500. The dog's wagging tail is 500. So, it isn't like the whole thing marches together. The intellect certainly is not the same in the kitty. The intellect is not the same. The intellect is not the same in the dinosaur and bin Laden, but they both calibrate the same level. How did they both come out 70? One's scaly and vicious, one is manifesting in physical form what it is; the other has disguised itself within a human. But it's the same energy, same energy. Same energy. It kills out of that viciousness which is part of that level of consciousness. So, we can't make it wrong. We can't say he is wrong. Can't say the dinosaur is wrong. Can't say the Middle East is wrong. We just notice that life evolves, and it evolves in that way.

So, first of all, you could let go wanting to change the world, and you can surrender it to God. Even if the world *is* the way you see it, you still have to allow God to be God. When it's time for you to become savior of the world, you'll be notified. But the question brings up, you know, that famous teaching of Ramana Maharshi. The reason I quote Ramana Maharshi and Nisargadatta Maharaj a lot is because they lived in recent years and what they said was taken down verbatim, so we know exactly what they said in response to certain questions. When you go back to gurus that are 2,500 years old, it's anybody's guess what they said or how it was interpreted. But you remember Ramana Maharshi said, "There's no point in trying to save the world, because the world that you perceive doesn't even exist." It's all projection of your own perception. And these are people working out their own salvation, and to you, that looks like . . . you know, I remember that lifetime; I've already recited some lifetimes in which I learned those lessons myself. So, you don't become a saint without being a pirate at one time, apparently. And a lot of the rather difficult lessons I've learned were lived through, so perhaps consciousness has to evolve through the lower chakras in order to get to the higher chakra.

Certainly, the intention of praying for the world has a collective benefit effect. Let's see if that's so: "This has a collective benefit effect: resist." [True.] It does have a collective benefit effect, but the motivation is different. The motivation to send one's love and forgiveness, et cetera, out into the world—you're not trying to control something, you see. So, the ego's into control, and the spiritual ego is into controlling people for pious-sounding reasons. But it's still control. If you want to control people for their own good, it's still wanting to control them, right? Like, you want to get them sober, right? Well, the first step in Al Anon is to let go wanting to control that which is out there, because it finds its own salvation. You may deprive them of the karmic benefit of evolving and evolving in the karmic merit of choosing. So, if you force somebody, you've robbed them of the karmic merit of making that choice, because one's level of consciousness is determined by choice, by the spiritual free will. So, if we force conditions, then, in a way we do a disservice spiritually, because the only reason they're doing that is because we have them locked up; that is not a choice on their part. They have not hit bottom about it. Sooner or later, you would think the Middle East would hit bottom, but that's probably fallacious. There's so much gratification and fun in all this—playing hero, victim, and perpetrator—that I doubt this game is going to quit for a long, long time. Besides, with people that have those lessons to learn, where else can they go on the planet to learn that? You can't overcome your fear of physical death until you actually walk into bullets. You've really got to walk into them, and then you pop out of body and you realize . . . (you're free).

One time on a slave ship, chained to this oar—the details are gory, and I don't want to go into it, but there were no latrines or anything else. Once in a while, when the guy that led the beat couldn't stand it anymore, they'd open all the portholes, and it was horrible. So, anyway, this torture and torment and being beaten up and all the rest, I finally reached the point that I could not push myself any further, and suddenly came like a light, "You're not trapped." I left the body. The dead body lay there. I was free as a bird, without enslavement, without torture. Without the extremity of the situation, I would have never had the courage to transcend it. Suddenly, like, a knowingness said, "You're free." I just let go wanting to be with the body, and it croaked, and I was free. End of torture, end of torment. Up yours! Well, I guess this was the first time I did the finger! They had to haul the dead body out and everything, so there!

So, you need slave ships and galleys, and you need torture chambers, and you need—you hate to say that, but I don't know why the ego is so resistant. This is a whole area for research. Why people have to hit such a bottom before they get a point, and sometimes the point is so simple. You say, "Nobody would have any trouble admitting about themselves if they were wrong about some simple, little thing." People practically go to the gallows rather than admit, you know, that they were—you know, they left the wrong change on the counter, or something. I mean, this and that, a super crisis. You've seen that in your own life, haven't you? People go to the extreme over some triviality.

So, there must be some great karmic lesson to be learned in what we witness out there. So, we witness what we think is happening out there. If these are 78 percent of the population below 200 on the Map, or 85, or whatever in the world it is, 78 percent now, I guess, these people all have to have a life. They have to live someplace, they have to have a job, they have to eat, they have to stay alive. So, all these people are going to lead these kinds of lifestyles. If you're driven by greed in the solar plexus, then you're going to become president of a giant corporation and milk it for the multimillions. You've got to have someplace to do that. You can't do that as a slave in a galley. I mean, that was not an opportunity there. That was not an opportunity. That was not an option. So, you probably reinvent yourself, karmically you reinvent yourself.

EVERYTHING IN THE UNIVERSE IS FREE CHOICE

Now, somebody asked me about causality and karma. Karma does not *cause* anything. You see, everything in the universe is free choice. Everything in the universe is free choice. You have to get off this delusion about causality. Causality is a hypothetical operant. Operant. A hypothetical operant. It exists only as a hypothetical operant; it's a tautology. It has no existence in reality. You can't show me any causality, anywhere. The only place causality exists is as a thought in your mind. You don't see anything causing anything there at all. Nothing's causing anything. It *is* that way; everything *is* what it is. And if it is what it is, it doesn't have to be caused, does it? Existence is sufficient evidence in and of itself. It doesn't require some hypothesis outside of itself, because existence does not require an explanation. It is its own explanation because it *is* it. I forgot what the question was. That question of causality keeps coming back. No, it had to do with karma and causality.

That karma, you know, the way I picture it in my mind—I actually don't picture it in my mind—how should we language this? Karma is like the accumulated energy field, like a computer chip. It's part of one's spiritual body that follows you around. You can reincarnate because that is favorable to certain karmic resolutions, or you may not incarnate. You may go to other domains and dimensions. There's an infinite number of dimensions. Let's see if that's so: "There's an infinite number of dimensions." [True.] "And one is karmically free to choose: resist." [True.] There's an infinite number of dimensions. People say, "Well, there's the earth, and then there's heaven and there's hell." Oh my God, there's an infinite number of dimensions, and they expand at an infinite rate. An infinite number of dimensions expanding at an infinite rate. At the rate of infinity, you might say. So, if the—let's say, the vibrational pill, no, the vibrational chip, the vibrational chip in your spiritual body then would vibrate at a certain frequency, and it gravitates toward that to which it is most perfect, huh? Just like a dandelion seed floats through the air depending on the waves and the wind and the humidity and how old it is, and the gravity, and it floats into a place that's just right, on top of a cherry tree leaf, which is not right if you want to be a dandelion. You can't grow on top of a cherry tree leaf. So, then another wind comes along, and, ooh, you go off the cherry tree leaf, and now you land down here, and you get born in Milwaukee, Wisconsin, and learn German in school. Everybody—then you get older, and you move away and forget your German. Then you wish you knew how to speak Spanish. Oh God.

[Q]: "What about the falling of people's calibration?"

We've already mentioned that. Karmic choices are constantly present. They're limited, they're limited. Karmic choices are limited by whatever domain you happen to be calibrated in, so for that reason, there's a limitation to freedom of choice. That's why we try to pick that which is appropriate, where the conditions are appropriate. You see, a giraffe is not given the opportunity to be a cat, you know what I'm saying? It's not within his choice. So, each karmic kernel, you might say, that is carried on into the next lifetime determines all these multiple things, and it does so almost like gravity, like wind currents on a seed.

[Q]: "Must one be at the depth of intolerable misery in order to fully surrender? What is the best way to accomplish this?"

I never asked this one. I really don't know why I did it. It has to reach such an unbearable degree. Maybe the more powerful the ego, the more powerful the ego. Some people have intensely powerful egos. Adolph Hitler had a very powerful ego. He's got, first of all, level of consciousness; he's got something else too. He's got charisma, but he's got a lot of power, because a lot of egomaniacs with political ambitions out there didn't succeed like he did in his realm. So, there seems to be, perhaps, a quantitative thing. It was never looked at. We were looking at a calibrated level, but were not looking at quantitative, so, okay, let's ask: "We have permission to ask: resist." [True.] "Besides the calibrated level, there is a quantitative aspect: resist." [True.] Wow. We never knew that before. I suspected it, I suspected it. How did I suspect it? We were asking the difference between reading the writings of a guru and actually being in their presence, and we got that there was a difference. Not on the calibrated level. The speaker at 620, his writings will be 620. But we got that there was greater benefit, and that it was not a calibratable benefit, but one of quantity. "So, it has to do with intensity." [True.] "Quantity." [True.] "Availability." [True.] "So, it would be analogous to, analogous to, uh, amperage: resist." [True.] Uh huh. "So, the calibrated level would be like the voltage." [True.] "But it's still a quantitative amperage." [True.] It's like amperage. Okay. So, what was the question?

I suppose, then, a resistance might be the same thing. There could be willy-nilly little resistances where you let it go, or there could be very, very powerful ones, evolved over great eons of time, that it takes the ultimate to break down. Let's see if that's so: "That is so: resist." [True.] Okay. Now, earthly life is also an opportunity we haven't tested: "I have permission to ask this question here in front of this audience: resist." [True.] "It's as I am seeing it in my mind: resist." [True.] So, entities from lower domains—I don't use that in a pejorative meaning. Entities from—we think life on our planet's bad; there are universes where this is heaven—reincarnate on this planet, so we get entities from other realms that

The Source of Our Existence Is Silence | 131

are really, really awful. So, when I said, a couple of sessions ago, that our world is really purgatorial—this is really, like, purgatorial, where you get to live out the karmic set from previous decisions, and where the gamut goes from the most awful to the highest. It goes from bin Laden to Jesus Christ. You see the enormous range of choices here. So, the freedom of being born a human on this planet, in this millennium, is the incredible multitude of choices, and I suspect in other domains there is not that range of choice: "That's a correct statement: resist." [True.] "So, they come here for the great range of freedom: resist." [True.] "This does not exist in other domains: resist." [True.] Yes. "I suspect other domains are ruled by powerful entities that limit choice: resist." [True.]

[Q]: "Why do you suppose some people must reach such incredible depth of unbelievable suffering and misery in order to surrender?"

I don't know if we'll be allowed to find the answer, but let's work on it. What do you think? "Of hopelessness"—you have to reach hopelessness, is that what he said? Yes. Why does it take him so long to reach hopelessness? I mean, after a guy's been jailed five times, his wife left him, they've taken off his right leg, he's blind and going deaf, and the guy says, "No, I don't wanna give up drinking yet," you think, "God almighty! What does it take, do I have to put his head in a thumbscrew?" You know, like this? I can see why the Inquisition arose, you know? What did you say? "That's the truth." [True.] Wow! Thank you. Yes, that makes sense, doesn't it? The desire to let it go must be equal to that which created it in the first place, huh. That's very good, very good. In other words, by merit. In other words, you're undoing it by merit, in a way. The desire has to be intense. People ask, "Why do some people reach enlightenment? They're all following the same pathway, following the same techniques, the same ashram, the same meditation. Why do some walk ahead and others don't?" The only answer I've ever seen or experienced was the intensity of the desire. It has to be voracious, almost inhuman, or ultrahuman, or metahuman. The intensity has to be ferocious to reach the goal. And that's how you break the barrier in any sport. For instance, when you hit the wall, you cannot go beyond. You cannot accept that limitation, and you, by sheer force of will, and you white-knuckle it and grit your teeth, and by sheer determination, you crash through. That's about what it takes to reach the higher levels of enlightenment. It has to be tenacious one-pointedness of mind, with a fixity of goal and intensity.

The willingness to let it all go and go back up like a cork in the water. Anybody got any other ideas why do some people have to hit such an incredibly horrible bottom before they let go? I believe that's so. Also, some people have the capacity to experience and survive suffering of amazing degrees, whereas other people, their tolerance is very, very minimal. I've seen patients in the office over the years, you know, and their complaints were . . . I can't imagine why they would get in a car and go see a doctor for that, you know what I'm saying? "I feel chilly when it's below zero." I mean, you know, is that a problem? "My nose runs when I've been out in the cold, and I get dandruff." Why is this person seeing a doctor, you know? Each person has their own threshold, and I suppose. . . . Don't forget, spiritual training, a lot of spiritual trainings are very severe. I've been through some that were, you know, about as far as you could handle. And it wasn't just EST either, without going to the bathroom. Made EST seem like a playground. Pretty severe. But even EST, you know, is the bottom for some people. You remember, those of you who did EST, the fact that you couldn't go to the bathroom when you had to? You saw people actually laying on the floor, screaming, and frenzies, and going into catatonic states of shock that they couldn't look at their watch or. . . . Not going to the bathroom, that was the big one. And not having any time off, no food. There's not going to be any lunch. No. Then there was a bunch of people on the floor, going into, you know, existential panic that they're going to die if they didn't eat, et cetera.

So, all of everybody's stuff came up, you know. Like you were saying, there's a great variety, some of which, to the observer, we would think is ridiculous, but to them it was really a crisis. I suppose if you were beaten up at age three months for wetting your panties, the fact that you can't go to the bathroom is going to bring up existential terror, and they are going to go through something that you won't go through. All right. So, we might say, inadvertently we all create our own bottom, inadvertently. We all create our own bottom by either conscious or unconscious decisions. And many decisions, as you do spiritual work, you become conscious of that you made them, but you'd forgotten them or they're unconscious. You obviously must. So, anything that's going on in your life, you can presume that was a choice, even though you'd say, "I'd never, never decide that. I would *never* decide that, I would never choose so-and-so." Oh yes, you would've under the right conditions. I say, "If you don't choose that, I'll blow your head off." Boy, you just made that decision in a hurry. The right conditions, you'd make any kind of a choice, any kind of agreement, pact with—*pact*—p, a, c, t, with whatever energies may be tempting you at the moment. And later on, in another lifetime, you say, "I never could have agreed to that."

It is a very good question, because you do wonder why people, other people have sort of a congenital capacity to handle greater pain. People have a lot higher and lower pain thresholds, which you can test out. And some people have very low pain thresholds. Experientially, I can tolerate things that are excruciating beyond probably 95 percent of the population's capacity. And anybody except an idiot would have given up long before I did, you know. The other thing is, people are trained to handle certain things, so if you've been trained to handle it without flinching, you can probably stand up there, you know, and get carved to death and not, you know, flinch, because you've been trained to do that. All right.

So, we'd say there's probably been some agreements made to which you are unaware. So, the best thing would be to presume that you made that choice and that you made that agreement. Shall we see? "That would be wise." [True.] "Operationally, it's best to presume that that is a choice and a decision that you made: resist." [True.] Operationally. Just the fact that you can't consciously recall it doesn't mean anything. Anybody who's been in psychoanalysis knows that. You've made a lot of decisions that were totally unconscious. And as they go through psychoanalysis, then it becomes conscious, and you realize that you made that decision because of the context at the time, because of its meaning at the time.

"What would Mother Teresa have said in Basha's parking lot?" In the next book, we'll be more into Mother Teresa. Because the talk is "The Way to God"—through devotion, through the heart, you know. Most of these lectures, we've been approaching it more like the Zen, more like nonduality, Advaita, whatever you call it. Well, how do you pronounce it? *Ad-vai-ta. Ad-vai-ta.*

So, we've been dissecting the mind, taking it apart, and one of the reasons we did it in this sequence is because, when the obstacles to love are removed, *shew*! It's sudden. The way to sudden enlightenment is to remove all the obstacles, and then you turn up the fire under the burner and, shew! So, everybody will be enlightened within 60 days. We've tried to do it in that way. I've noticed the *Course in Miracles* did it in the same way. I was fascinated by the *Course in Miracles* because, before presenting you with the truth that "I am love, and I am spirit, and God and I are one," et cetera, long before that, it first disassembles the ego. First, it takes the ego out, which is going to say, "This is nonsense. This wouldn't apply to me, I'm just a nobody." First it says, you know, "My thoughts don't mean anything." Whoa. That was a brilliant move. When I saw that lesson, I said, "This is spiritual genius; this is written by a spiritual genius." To see that the sequence should be to first disassemble the ego before you present it with spiritual truth. Religion does it the other way. It presents you with spiritual truth at a point where you couldn't possibly grasp that that's a reality. You've got so much guilt, you couldn't own that for yourself. You've got so much shame, you couldn't possibly do it. You've got so much annoyance at God, who's going to punish you later, and you're so scared of him, you hate him. Religion doesn't have a chance with the average person, you know. You've got to talk yourself into believing it, and that's what's called "faith." Despite all of the irrationality of it, you know, you go with it.

But for a spiritual seeker, then, the correct sequence is to first comprehend the nature of the ego, how it got to be that way, so that you can own it. You can't own the ego if you're going to go into guilt, shame, see it as your enemy, hate it, fear it, et cetera. Some spiritual pathways do that. They set up the ego as an enemy, uh, and reinforce it. So, by familiarity we take the ego apart, you know, stick by stick, like pickup sticks. We see how it does this, creates a bifurcation; then we go back to the source of the bifurcation. We surrender that. The bifurcation and all the multiple bifurcations that come off of that decision now all disappear. All the algorithms, you know. One choice creates a duality. Each branch of the duality now bifurcates until you've got thousands and thousands of your neurons all jumping with hating the bastard. Bin Laden, you want to kill him, he's awful, he's evil, he's terrible, he's—see, all that stuff—the guy doesn't know what he's doing, does he? He's a mental case, right? To be brainwashed into the exact opposite of spiritual truth, there's got to be a few nuts and bolts missing, you know what I'm saying.

So, if we disassemble the ego by understanding its structure—so, if you want to take something apart, you understand how it's put together. If you understand how it's put together, now you can start taking the sticks out. And the structure becomes weaker and weaker, weaker and weaker. Then you come in with the fire of the heart after all the obstacles have been removed that would've already eliminated it or deterred you from even following the pathway of devotion.

* * *

So, in these lectures, we started with the basic underpinning of the ego, which is the belief in causality. We worked our way through how dualistic thinking arises and how to let go of the positionality, because it only creates a whole other set of dualities, each branch of which then creates a whole other set of dualities, and you can pull the pin on the whole bank of it, see. Millions of neurons—the minute you pull the pin on this one, *shwttt*, they go silent. All that chitchat stops. So, that's the reason we presented this in the sequence that it has. So, this is number eight. And I think the way of the heart is number nine. And having seen that the obstacles were all artifacts of mentalization with no intrinsic reality, we can easily dispense with them. At that point, then, spiritual commitment, intensity, what it takes to break the four-minute mile, now will have a chance to succeed without all those impediments in their way, yeah? So, first we tried to remove the obstructions before we turned up the fire. That's the reason for the sequence of the lectures.

If you start with, "You should be loving God," you start with, as many religions do, to love God, the heart of Jesus, the statues, the whole thing, you feel compelled to love on a level which your ego will not allow you to love at. If you could love at that degree, you'd already be there. So, it puts—it seems to me that that is putting the cart before the horse. Before you pressure people to become loving, you have to remove the obstructions without which they would automatically become loving, because the presence of God within you expresses itself as Divinity expresses itself: as Universal Love. So, we try to remove the obstacles, and then lovingness becomes a real possibility. Too often it becomes an artificial self-belief. I hear all kinds of people telling me how pious they are and how loving they are. Yeah, right, until it comes to your mother, right, until it comes to your mother-in-law, your ex-wife, right. Exceptions start coming up. So, that degree of lovingness that one wishes to arrive at is obstructed by the ego, so we're trying to disassemble the ego.

So, intention. A lot of spiritual work comes out the solar plexus. It's ambition, spiritual ambition. So, it's sort of a solar-plexus drive, you see what I'm saying? It's coming out of the solar plexus. So, a lot of driven kind of spirituality, which some branches of some churches over time, you know, despite the severe degrees, are coming out of the solar plexus. It's got nothing to do with love, you see. And so, you keep—you know, "We're going to put you on the rack and keep it going until you agree to love God." It's the nature of the Self, with a capital *S*, within. It's not different than that which is Love. And to merely remove its obstacles allows the love to shine forth. The Divinity of the Self within is unmistakable. And as it shines forth, it begins to radiate much like the dawn.

As the decision to be loving is a decision, it's Love. It's not within the realm of Reason. This is Logic: logic would tell you, "Love that guy? He should be in jail." "Love him? He's a criminal!" What am I saying? Reason would tell you that it's ridiculous to love all these ways that you're supposed to love. And then you go to church, and you're supposed to have a loving heart and love your neighbor as yourself. How can you love your neighbor as yourself when he's such a creep? So, you pretend he's not really a creep. That's a lie; he *is* a creep. You run him on the creep index, bzzz! bzzz! bzzz! bzzz! He's a creep. Everybody in the neighborhood thinks he's a creep. He *is* a creep. Reason says, "He—is—a—creep. I hate him, and I feel guilty about hating him. I feel sad that he moved into my neighborhood, and I hate him so much. I'm afraid that he may have retaliatory homicidal fantasies toward me, which throws me into Paranoia. However, out of Courage, I'm pleased with myself that I faced up to him and told him, 'If you don't stop whatchamacallit, I'm going to call the police.'" This moves me right back down to Paranoia again. You see, Reason isn't too much of a help right here. It keeps throwing us back and forth into this basket.

THE WILLINGNESS TO LOVE NO MATTER WHAT

So, the willingness to love, no matter what, is really a pact you're making with God. Really a pact you're making with God. "I choose to be with Thy Will, O Lord, and love unconditionally." So, this is a choice, made by conscious decision—not out of logic, but because you're already evolved enough that that contract is now compelling. You realize it's going to have a big cost. You realize it's going to make a cost. Anybody who chooses to be unconditionally loving knows in that contract, it's going to be a price. All that which is unloving is going to come up to be surrendered. On the other hand, you now get assistance from dimensions from which you never got assistance before. Let's see if that's so: "We have permission to ask this question." [True.] "What I just said is so." [True.] Oho! See, the contract has now brought in powers from other dimensions which you did not have before. So, when you're trying to become unconditionally loving from down here in the ego, you haven't got the power that it takes to become unconditionally loving, so you keep falling back into despair. And you see spiritual histories throughout time of various saints, how they would go into a high state, then they would fall. "Oh, my Beloved, how could you have deserted me?" There in the presence of the bliss of the Presence, and then suddenly it disappears, and they crash into severe dark nights of the soul. The dark night of the soul is from trying to push the envelope. You're trying to push the unconditional love when you haven't let go of what is holding you back from unconditional love. Consequently, I tell everybody, "Stop trying to be loving. Give me a break, will you?" "Stop trying to be loving. You're putting a pressure on me, on you, on everybody." Quit trying to be loving. It either occurs of its own, or it does not. And any forced kind of love is going to be artificial. It's going to lack within it the security system, you see? Because love's going to lead you into dangerous situations. Without the help of unseen helpers, you're not going to be able to handle the seas at that, you understand? There's no point to force yourself, because when the time is ready, it becomes the way you are automatically.

You walk through the alley, the beetle's laying on its back. He needs help. You either squish him—that was a shock to do that. You squish him or you say. . . . The last time I did it, the idiot turned back on his back again. "Geez, what's the matter with you?" I put the twig on him again. He went over on his back again. I said, "There's some message here I'm not getting. I'm trying to exert *my* will on him and make him choose life." Sure enough, when I came back an hour later, he was dead. I asserted my will to the beetle's will. He wanted to leave this body and go get himself a new body because the old one was all worn out; you know what I mean. He probably went on the other side and reincarnated in another, and he's probably back and flying around already. Is he back flying around already? Let's see: "We have permission to ask this question." [True.] "He's back flying around already." [True.] By God, he is. I knew he was going to turn right around, get reborn in an egg, and be out there flying again.

LIFE IS NOT SUBJECT TO DEATH

Life is not subject to death. That's one of the most profound things we've said in all these lectures. "Life is not subject to death: resist." [True.] Life is not subject to death. Something of its own quality. It takes something of its own power, its own quality to kill it. Nothing has the power to kill life. You cannot kill anything, you cannot kill life. What you can do is block its expression in this particular form and force it to choose another form, but you cannot kill life. Did you ever chop up a bowl of mercury? It's illegal nowadays. You're not allowed to chop up bowls of mercury. But when I was a kid, you know, Dad would always bring home mercury, and little kids—you know, you try and pick it up, and of course it would instantly go jiggly. And put a knife down it—no matter what you did, you could not break up this little pool of mercury. It was just mysterious and wonderful. Nowadays, it would probably get you arrested; the EPA would be around there, ringing your doorbell. You're getting mercury vapors out into the world, or something. In those days there was really freedom, and you could poison yourself if you wanted, you know. Which is something else you don't have to worry about, because as we've demonstrated before, the time of your death is already set. Let's reaffirm: "At the time of birth, the exact time of your death is already karmically set: resist." [True.] "The style and the manner of it is not set, correct." [True.] The style and the manner of your death is not set. That, you have many choices. But the timing is already set. What can you say about that? It means you're completely and totally free. And what is set is the time, you know, karmically set, in which you're going to change form. You're going to come out of this form, and you're going to go into a different form, where other choices are waiting, et cetera. So, there's no point in worrying about what you eat and how you eat it, and what you do and all, because when you're going to leave here, you're going to leave here.

I knew a guy—I've told you, his father was 92 years old, and he was standing on the street corner in Cottonwood, in perfect health, God bless him. And a cement truck came and *bam*, smacked him deader than a mackerel. He should have kept on drinking the brandy and smoking the cigars and eating the roast beef, you know what I'm saying? And his son was saintlike, and he said, "No, I'm not going to sue this cement company." He said: "That driver feels terrible. It was a real accident. Why should I sue him?" I thought that was very evolved. That he accepted it, you know, like God's Will, and he saw the innocence of the driver. He said the driver certainly didn't will that; the last thing the driver said to himself that morning—"I think I'll kill an old man on the street corner." Within human error. So, our willingness to forgive others for human error is part of our own salvation. And as the son said that to me, I got the feeling of his spiritual destiny, in a way. He just was going to be a saint. I mean, he was almost a saint already.

And you meet saints in your life, you know, but it's not popular to think of them as saints, but there are. You can break down on the highway and a complete stranger will do all kinds of things for you; run all over, spend hours and all kinds of trouble, go and get you a spare tire and drive you back and wake his buddy up who owns a tire company, and brings it back. This is all four in the morning. You say, "What could this be?" Let's see: "We have permission to ask that: resist." [True.] "That was an angelic person: resist." [True.] Yeah. So, we also have angelics. Who would, but an angel, would do a thing like that? And I thought, "My God, this guy's actually an angel in a physical body. Some kind of a helper angel. "He was: resist." [True.] Thank God he was an angel in a physical body.

What does an enlightened person do when a robber's going to blow you away? Says, "I'm going to kill you!" What does an enlightened person do? He goes, "I don't mind being killed." You know, you shoot out of body and you're in an incredible space, but that loud noise, man . . . I just hate that loud noise. Okay, so, let's put our fingers in our ears and pray for the best, and we'll meet again after a short break.

"We have permission to do this: resist." [True.] "We have permission to do this: resist." [True.] Okay. Most of the great teachers of recent times, very well-known, some American—mostly they teach in the high—they usually get in the high 500s. The ideal level for a teacher would be the high 500s; it would be the perfect level. First of all, lower, you don't have enough power for the power of your words to go through the ego's resistances. Beyond 600, you're not very useful in the world. Beyond 590, you're not very useful in the world. You can sit there and bless people as they walk by, in a bliss state. That's about all you can do. And I recommend that you continue doing that. You get blissed out, sitting on a rock? Stay there. Yeah. I tell you, what pulls you out of those 500 states is love, because you have a love relationship that would be impacted by your sitting on the rocks, out of your love. So, that's an attachment to love. Love itself, if it was perfected, you'd sit on the rock. Okay.

So, a lot of the famous teachers, you know, we call them saints. The one who was recently canonized by the Vatican, Father Pio, yeah, Father Pio. I don't speak Latin. Father Pio, anyway, yes, is probably 580, 590. He's very evolved, very high 500s. So, those are the great teachers, really of the high 500s: Yogananda; the pope is at 570; the Dalai Lama's at 570. To run a huge, worldwide church, you can't be much beyond 570 and still do it. See, so each one is perfect for that which he is. If you want to be the great beneficence—let's say, the current pope, who images people to get together and share love, brotherhood, and Christianity with each other. He's a great peacemaker. So, to run a great church, should be in the high 500s, 570. Saints are really 570 to 590, 595. So, we would expect saintlike people. Kriya yoga—I forget; kriya yoga, I think, is in the 400s. "520" [True.] "530." [True] "540." [Not true.] 540. Kriya yoga's 540.

So, let's understand what the calibrations mean. What the calibration means is, each technique is for a purpose and appeals to you at a certain time, and therefore, it's perfect. To choose a technique that calibrates at 800 when you're at 300 is not going to work. If you're at 350, I would choose one about 380, 400, a teacher at 420, because you're still getting the basics. It's important to get the basics, and so, it's not that 600 is better than—it's not better than; it's different than. So, we learn the basic skills, so your best teacher would be somebody who appeals to you that you can bond with, who's meaningful to you, with whom you feel a certain compatibility. So, that's the best teacher.

The style that somebody of a much higher calibration has may not appeal to you at all, you see. So, I would choose that which you feel compatible with. What you want to know: Is it integrous?

And the exact calibration doesn't mean anything. Why? Because you can take a simple technique, any simple concept or technique, and if you follow it relentlessly without one single omission—never once are you allowed to . . . if you follow kindness toward yourself and all living things, no matter what, without exception, with a fixity of purpose, that'll take you the whole way. You understand? So, it isn't so much the calibration of the teaching as the degree to which one commits to it. "Easy does it." "Live and let live." "First things first." Those are all very powerful. You put those into operation, you're going to be at—what is the 12-step work? That at 540? 540, yeah. All right. So, even the 12 steps of the 12-step program, if you follow that relentlessly, you're looking at 540, which is Unconditional Love. Unconditional Love, somebody can rip you off for 20,000 dollars, and that was yesterday. What did he do to me today? Nothing! Unconditional Love means no matter what happens, but there at 540, you see the vulnerability for that which is nonintegrous to come into your life. And so, although you have the capacity to forgive the headsman, you know, as your head is there, you're praying for the guy who shouldn't feel guilty for chopping your head off. That's 540. That's what I do; those that chop my head off, I pray for the guy: "That's a fact. [True.] I knew it. Okay. So, the willingness to forgive the headsman, then, is coming from the heart, and is a fulfillment of the choice to be loving toward all things, *no matter what*, you see? It doesn't mean you've got to forgive everybody, but the headsman you're going to hate, or Hitler you're going to hate, or somebody, you're going to make an exception. You cannot make any exception.

So, it isn't how high the teacher is, or the teaching is, but your commitment to it, because what gives it its power—its power has several sources. One is your level of commitment to it. I'm sure in

India, to turn the prayer bells, relentlessly day after day after day, may seem ridiculous to a Western mind, but think of the degree of commitment. Haha, and you have to give money to the church to do this too, put your money in there to crank the bells, the prayer bells. We'd say, "Well, that's ridiculous, you know, cranking prayer bells. I mean, does God hear prayer bells clanking up there in heaven and give you merit? But think of the amount of dedication to that, and then because—so, anything can be your way to God. Anything can be your way to God.

So, it isn't—the technique tells you where it fits into an overall scheme of things, but it doesn't tell you how beneficial it would be to you. I already told you the truth when you came in here, and none of you got enlightened that instant, did you? I told you, there's nothing happening, nobody here, nothing's being said, and there's no mind to hear it or speak it. I already told you that. That's 999; that's the truth. That's a fact. Knowing that is no help, is it? Maybe it makes you feel worse, you know what I'm saying? Yeah, it makes you feel worse.

[Q]: "How could we live through the intense, constant pain of physicality when we are in the 600s?"

Well, you can live through constant pain. Physical pain is a thing that comes up very often, and physical pain takes you through all kinds of learning processes, takes you through alternate treatment methods—it takes you through acupuncture, it takes you through hypnosis, it takes you through mantras and physicalities and prayings and all kinds of things. And learning how to disregard it, learning how to disregard it.

See, suffering is one thing; pain is another. That's what's really being asked. There's pain, but once you let go resisting pain—I told you how to let go suffering from pain, right? Remember? I'll go through it once again, but suffering is one thing and pain is another. When the suffering leaves the pain, you ignore the pain, because you're not suffering from it anymore, you understand? Suffering means you haven't processed it out. You're resisting it. Physical pain, one lets go resisting it; stops running away from it, trying to avoid it. Stop trying to control it. If you do that, the pain goes from local to diffuse. You can feel, like, your whole aura: the pain from your twisted ankle now is everywhere around you. You keep surrendering to it and let go resisting to it. You can't resist for even a split second, or you feel the pain again. You let go resisting it continuously. Within a matter of minutes, it fades out and you get up and walk away. Nothing to it. It's just a willingness to do that. And to get through excruciating pain, you can't relent for even a split second, or the pain overwhelms you, it shocks you, you almost pass out from it. So, that's what you do: you let go resisting. So, pain is one thing; suffering is another. Anybody who's been in pain and had a narcotic remembers that. They give you a shot of morphine—the gallbladder, the pain is still there, but you're not suffering from it, because you're in a different space. You are what you are and the pain is what it is, but you are not the pain. So, that's what morphine does for you. It doesn't eliminate the pain. You say, "Is the pain there?" "Yeah, it's still there." But you are not suffering from it, so suffering is one thing, pain is another.

There's an infinite number of dimensions. We said that this really takes us into advanced theoretical physics and quantum theory to be able to comprehend. Um, at every instant, an infinite number of potentialities is, you might say, becomes actualizable, becomes, uh, ac—actual—I can't say it. Every instant, there is released an infinite number of potentialities. Each of those potentialities, in turn, releases an infinite number of potentialities, which in turn releases an infinite number of potentialities. There is, therefore, at all times, an infinite number of dimensions, an infinite number of dimensions. "We have permission to ask that at this time: resist." [True.] "There is an infinite number of dimensions: resist." [True.] "And they are expanding at an infinite rate: resist." [True.] That is beyond the human imagination to comprehend. At every instant, an infinite number of potentialities are releasing an infinite number of potentialities, which each in turn releases another infinite series of potentialities. If I send out 10,000 sparks, each spark can send out 10,000 more, of which each spark can create 10,000 more, and it happens at the speed of light. "It happens beyond the speed of light: resist." [True.] Because while I'm talking—this is in the physical domain. There's an infinite number of, you see . . . and theoretical physics and astronomy are discovering there's an infinite number of galaxies with an infinite number of planetary systems. An infinite number of galaxies, and the galaxies are expanding, you know, at the speed of light, but there are dimensions beyond the speed of light which expand and multiply beyond the speed of light. That ought to give those neurons something to do, eh? [holds forehead and wobbles] Just to think it has knocked me out of my chops here. Yeah, and you hear people thinking they're greater than God. I think, "Yes, right, uh huh." An infinite number of dimensions expanding at faster than the speed of light, and an infinite number . . . and you're bigger and more powerful than that.

[Q]: "What can you do if you break into tears in the presence of beauty?"

Get a box of Kleenex, is what I'd do. But that's that point that you reach in spiritual evolution where the innocence, the beauty, and the holiness of everything knocks you out of the box. And it's true, it's difficult; that's why we say a world religious leader can't handle—can't really handle it at 580 or 590, because at 580 or 590, you break into tears over everything: the beauty of the pattern of the rug, the magnificence of every animal. Every animal that walks by knocks you out. This morning I'm looking for kitty, and there's a raccoon, just as adorable as it could be, on the edge of the tree, whoa! I mean, the raccoon knocked me out, you know what I'm saying? He didn't care I was there. He sort of went into a swoon, sort of, just like the deer do when we talk about the deer. We talked about the deer the last time, didn't we? You see the deer. The animal gets how much you love it, and that does not mean you can put your head in its mouth [laughter], because it may just love you so much, it could just eat you up! So, you don't want to tempt it, you don't want to tempt it and push its love beyond its capacity.

So, the high 500s, then, are the realm of the great teachers. Their intention is integrous. Their wish is to energize the capacity to love in everyone, to share their insights so that people can overcome the obstacles to that lovingness. And if everybody gets to 540, you've got no worry, I'll tell you. "500 and above, you've got no worries: resist." [True.]

That's right, 500 and over, you've got no worries. Because that which is loving gravitates into, as it leaves the body, that which is compatible with that lovingness. It is not attracted to that which is down there; it's attracted to beauty. You find in your own life, as people get more evolved, they tend to seek more and more rural areas, less and less noise, less and less activity. Very often, life comes to a complete stop. The person says, "I am not *doing* anything in the eyes of the world." And I think, "Fantastic!" Because not being run by doingness, you know, is genuflecting at the knee of the doer within you. The doer is very useful. The doer will take you out of apathy, up through the solar plexus, into rajas, into high rajas, and then eventually you go into tranquility and sattva, and at that point, doingness is no longer a necessity. Also, there's the discovery that there is no doer doing anything. Doingness is happening of its own. So, you neither take credit for it, nor do you blame yourself for it. There is no thinker behind the thinkingness. The thinkingness is thinking itself. The doingness is—the action is activating itself, and you'll see that the actions of the body are like a karmic windup toy. It's all set to do that. There's no one to take credit for it, or discredit. The illusion that there is— you see, that's the source of the belief in causality—that there is a "something," a "some person," a "who" that is secretly controlling all of this. This is the old homunculus sitting in the back of your brain, pulling all those switches, and there is an operations center within the ego that integrates an enormously complex series of functions. When I talk about it—I forget, *The Eye of the I* or *I*, I forget which—there is this operations center where, when you look at what the human mind is asked to do, no computer could come anywhere near it. Millions of multiple options decided, you know, chosen in pathways, from instant to instant; all within a feelingness complex because all decisions, thoughts, and feelings are also filed in the memory file according to feeling tone. The complexity is mind-boggling. Together with unconscious factors, together with energies within the field, of which you have no knowingness; together with enormous complexity of programs coming from past karmic momentum, no computer could even get near it. Could not get near it, because it's not within the realm of logic, because the entire field shifts every time context shifts in the slightest. The whole field shifts, and nothing that you're even into is even applicable; then if the field shifts a little bit, it's all nonsensical. That's the purpose of humor. I never trust anybody that doesn't have a sense of humor. They're dangerous. They're killers. All killers are humorless.

We just stepped on a scorpion in the back. We were talking about "is there death?" There was this big scorpion, which now, to me, was not integrous, because if you get a scorpion sting on the tail, it can be fatal, you know what I'm saying? "That was integrous." [True.] "The scorpion is dead: resist." [True.] "This scorpion is dead." [True.] "Scorpion-ness is dead: resist." [True.]

So, the decisions that we make, the intention behind them is what sets the karmic energy field going. Um, the same action out of revenge or hatred has a different karmic consequence than, let's say, to protect one's integrity. To kill out of anger, fear, revenge, or greed is a totally different act than defending one's homeland, let's say, which you have no choice. You have a wife and a family and children, and the Huns are coming over the horizon with their scimitars flashing, and uh . . . they always, they always kill everybody they conquer. That was tradition; in the great hordes of history, they always killed everybody. You massacred all of them. And you took the loot. And that's why slavery was an advance in consciousness, because suddenly, humans had a value. "Hey, we won't kill them; we'll sell them." So, whether slavery is one way or slavery is the other depends on which direction you look at it. Whether you shift to the past and look at it toward the future, or project yourself in the future and look back at the past.

That's why, to save the world, you're taught—you know, what Ramana Maharshi was saying is that all you can be working on is your illusion about your own perceptions. There's no such thing exists—is it an advance or is it a cruelty depends on how you look at it. To be a slave on a slave ship, on a galley, in a state of advanced agony was what? Horrible? Yeah, horrible. And then was taking the great chance. I could leave the body. I wasn't sure if there was a spirit. I had to let go that which is known: I'm a physicality—to the intuitive suggestion that was an intuition: that one is a spirit. Free as a bird! Ha, so was being chained to a galley a horrible event, or was it the doorway to enlightenment? Because that was the first lifetime of discovering conscious memory that one is actually a spirit, that that which I am rose up out of the physicality, and they had to drag it away.

So, behind that which you think is a thinker, a thinkingness is a thinker: there is no thinker there, so you don't have to worry about the thinker, because there isn't any. You just look at the thinking itself, and we try to transcend the blocks to enlightenment by understanding the nature of the construction of the ego.

* * *

Well, this is something we have addressed in previous lectures and we have addressed quite a bit in the books, a lot of them. A lot of attention given to it in the books. How the ego comes into being and how it gains its structure. The ego cannot discern the difference between an abstract concept and reality. That's why an abstract concept is one thing. It doesn't have any real concordant reality that's really a parallel confirmation. It's doesn't really—this does not flow into this; this flows parallel to it.

So, we should go more into causality. The mind thinks in terms of abstractions, then thinks that if it can be nominalized, given a word, a name, therefore it has existence. We can call things "transformation"; we can call them all kinds of things. Is such a thing happening in reality? No, it's happening in my mind. This is an abstract conceptualization. One of the most difficult things about transcending the mind is transcending the belief that concepts represent an independent reality, some kind of objective reality. If you go out there, no such thing exists out there. It doesn't exist. You can look all over the world and never find causality, because causality exists only as an abstract concept in your head. You'll just keep projecting that abstract concept over and over again onto everything you see. All that means is, you're projecting that thought, that argument, that concept onto the world, over and over again.

When I was young, I always had a hard time with homesickness and leaving any place, and I would mourn it. Even if I'd lived in a cardboard box under a bridge that said "Kleenex" on it, camp out there for a couple of weeks, I would mourn it. I really missed my big Kleenex box. I had everything arranged in there just the way I wanted it, with the little windows and cardboard and all, you know. I had a stone fort as a kid. Then they came along and moved all the stones; they were going to make something with it. I mean, I always got attached to wherever I lived. Home. It was home. Home is where the heart is, so my heart would be wherever I lived. In the depths of not having money, which at the time we could call poverty nowadays, I suppose. In the depths of not really having any cash, you could live in some rather miserable places. And then, when you left them, grieve all over again with homesickness for a little one-and-a-half-room up on the roof of somebody's house. So, it was so painful, it took me a long time to, like—it was just like homesickness; if you've ever been homesick, you know that feeling. So, I learned that that was painful, so if I moved, I would rent a new place and I would pay the rent on the old place so that I could move back there if I couldn't stand this homesickness. I paid rent on two places. If in a couple of months I couldn't stand it, I could always move back there. The knowingness that I could move back if I wanted eased the pain. This happened over and over again, every place I left. I would go through this pain of loss, heartbreak like losing a lover, you know. It was the homesickness of the child, for instance. So, home was a very, very special place. And one time, here I am leaving this huge estate, you know, which was really spectacular, really a showplace, in a way. And as I leave that, I realize [claps hands], "I'm going to project that sense of at-homeness onto the next place I go." It's in *me*, not in *it*. Each place I lived, *I* projected the sense of home, safety, love, familiarity; it came from *me*. I'll do it all over again for the rest of my life. If I have to move from where I am now, the next place will become special all over again, right? As soon as you move in, you fix it all up, now it's special. It's got the magic touch of yourself there. So, the feeling of being at home, comfort, security, and all that goes with homeness, which derives from childhood, got projected onto every place that you live. You project it there. It's not there. If we take a microscope and we take a whatchamacallit meter and take every molecule of that home apart, you will not find feeling-at-homeness there. That's from the heart, you understand?

The same with causality. Everything you see, because you see sequence in the world, you then—your mind jumps in and projects the concept of causality: "this" is causing "that." "This" is causing "that." In reality, what you see is the sequence of perception as Creation unfolds itself this way, you understand? So, there's nothing causing the hand to unfold; it has, innate within it, potentiality. Then a person says, "Yes, but isn't there an 'I' causing it by intention?" Today's lecture has to do with how to transcend duality. That is duality, per se: that there is an "I" causing an "it" through some magical modality called "causality." And that is the trap of the mind: to believe in the reality of these three factors. First of all, there's nothing happening out there, nor is there causality, nor is there any intrinsic independent entity called "I" to be causing it, hm? All things come into being by the unfoldment of the potentiality of Creation, and as it is witnessed sequentially to perception, one thinks that this is causing that. If you take that one point of observation out of time and space, then there is no sequence to which you would be ascribing the magical quality called "causality." If we back up the movie and you see the lady running backward, you say, "What's causing her to run backward?" Well, she's not running backward. That's only perception, you see?

You see that the concept "happening" in itself is an illusion. There is nothing "happening." There's nothing happening now; there's nothing happening now; "something" didn't happen a minute ago. "Something" is not about to happen now either. Why? All right. You have perception. Arbitrarily, I could say, "We start now, and we end now." That's a happening. Or I could say, "No, we'll start now, and we'll keep it going there." That's a happening. We can start at nine o'clock this morning and go on to four o'clock this afternoon. "Oh boy, that's a seven-hour happening." Well, we could start from 9 to 9:01. That was a happening.

Yoko Ono used to specialize in happenings. A bonfire would go off with rockets at midnight in the East Village somewhere. She chose to start it there and end it there. No, I say the happening was when she set up the bonfire stuff, and the happening continued until after the police left. That was a happening. A policeman would say, "It began to happen after she ran this bonfire. We got there, caught them red-handed." That's the start of the happening to *him*. "Then we took them off to jail." That's the end of the happening. "And I booked her." That's the end of the happening. To the lawyer, that's only the start of the happening: "She got taken off to jail. That's a violation of her civil rights. No, no. It started from there, and it's going on until right now, and I will defend her in court. She was only expressing the First Amendment. Expressing her freedom to create." You understand?

We project, then, "this" onto the world and say, "It's out there," whereas it's "in here." Understand? There is no "happening" anywhere. There is no "I" person causing the happening. There is no "causality" to account for. This arm has the potentiality to do that. Let's say, if I choose a pattern off an infinite number of patterns—if I choose this pattern, this arm automatically does this. And if I choose this other pattern, it automatically does this. If I choose this pattern, it does this.

So, by choice we release certain potentialities. By choice, what you see within the seed is the whole program of it defining its potentiality in terms of nonlinear potentiality. See, causality is looking within the Newtonian linear domain, which always sees a happening with a beginning, a cause, and an end; a consequence; et cetera. That's a very limited paradigm of reality. It won't take you to the dimensions that you go through, because the minute you get beyond logic, the 400s, these things are not even valid questions anymore.

Once you get to the 500s and you're talking about love, you're talking about quality now; it's not measurable. It doesn't start here and end there. Can't package it. There isn't any love meter. It's beyond definition by logic. A person says, "Yes, but I want love to fit into a comfortable box of thinkingness and logic." And so, we make futile attempts; poetry probably gets the closest: "How do I love thee? Let me count the ways." When I was a kid, I thought, "Boys don't like poetry, pfft!" How do I love thee, let me count the ways? Give me a break! Eight-year-old boys just loathe that kind of stuff. So, that which is seen as so beautiful and lovingness is a turnoff. Every eight-year-old says, "Awful! Women and girls like that." You know what I'm saying? See, so it doesn't even have any reality. . . . See, it doesn't even have any reality, or he'd be forced to accept that it's beautiful and loving. No, he has choice.

So, the minute we get beyond the confines of logic, which is based on definition, we're in a different domain. So, what we're doing here is stretching epistemology. Another one of the ways to God is to follow epistemology to its final, ferocious end. When you crash through from epistemology—how do we "know" and how do we know that we know? You make up a concept called "causality." How do you know that you know what causality even is? It's just a word. It's just a tautology. Well, "cause" is anything you want to call it, isn't it? It's just T, A, U, T. The string is taut now. "Cause" is anything you want to call it. You could say love is the "cause" of these people behaving this way. It's not the cause; it's the field. It's in that field that you're making certain choices that are really answerable in a way to the field of love, because that now is the context of truth and value. Outside of love, the world of business—we were talking about it during the break—business doesn't give a diddly about love. You're not even allowed to engage in love during lunch breaks, much less on the premises, please.

Touchy-feely is not, you know, cool in the business world. Being cool and logical is cool in the business world. So, the minute you get out of the dimension, then—we need our scale of consciousness again. The minute we get out of the 400s, then, causality becomes less and less meaningful. What does it mean up here [high on MoC]? It doesn't mean anything. In the field of love, joy, and peace, it doesn't even come up as a credible possibility. Nothing is *causing* you to feel peace. In this room, there's absolute silence. Behind all the noise, there's absolute silence. Remove the noise, and there's nothing here but silence, correct? Nothing is *causing* the silence. Nothing is causing your existence. Everything is free choice. Out of the Unmanifest comes the manifest. Out of that, all things are created with the one, single essential quality of existence. Within that existence, combined with form, you have an infinite series of potentialities. Nothing is causing it to happen. So, if we put a seedling, a rose seedling in the sun and give it water and fertilizer, the sun and the water and the fertilizer do not cause it to grow. The seed does not cause it to grow. It doesn't cause it. Cause, you see, is really within the world of force. The world of power here is different. From 200 down we have the world of force, in which one thing *forces* something else. That's not "cause"; that's force. "Cause"—you'd have to be divine, huh? These things are manifesting the choice of that as a potentiality.

Built within the human is the capacity to begin to vibrate at the energy of the kitty's purr, the doggie's wagging tail, and those are often the first things we love. That's why we give children pets and the toys and the fuzzy, warm things, because they begin to grasp their capacity of lovingness, and then they get attached to that which are loving, and they grieve and go into loss, and then they learn that they can re-create the same feeling about the next toy, and then they've transcended the attachment to love, the attachment to love, which also becomes a block.

I just want you to see that causality is an illusion, a powerful illusion. It's the whole basis of the ego; that's why it's so powerful and why it takes a lot of prayer and inner spiritual work to transcend it. All of a sudden, you see that everything is happening of its own. Nothing is causing anything to happen. The world of phenomena, the universe of Creation is like a giant electromagnetic field. All things within it have a certain charge, a certain energy, a certain polarity, like little iron filings with a north pole and a south pole, and a certain spin, and a certain degree of magnetic energy composed of various elements, and where it is in this space with billions and billions of others, automatically allows it to move within the realm of possibilities, like the aurora borealis. You see the aurora borealis; nobody is causing it to do what it's doing. The poles of the earth send out that electromagnetic, and you see—everybody here's seen the aurora borealis? You see how they dance—the pattern dances itself spontaneously as interaction between that which it is and the universe in which it is located. Nothing is causing anything to happen.

We spent some time on causality because it is so intrinsic to the structure of the ego. To merely begin to question causality as some kind of an intrinsic reality already weakens its power in holding the ego together. It's already weakened just by questioning its authenticity. It has no objective, substantial, substantive reality of its own.

The only reality that can be confirmed is a subjective state called "I." The presence of God within oneself, the Self with a capital S, which illuminates itself into your awareness as the feelingness that there's an "I," and that "I" exist, that's the only reality that you actually know. Beyond that is all imagination. Other than that you exist, there's no confirmable knowledge that you can possibly hold. Everything else then is a hypothetical possibility. Every piece of data the mind holds is a hypothetical abstraction. The only verification of reality, then, is the state of subjectivity. The only radical objective truth, then, is subjectivity itself. Without the subjective, no objective could be said to exist, because what would say that it exists? Only the subjective sense of Self says an objective reality is out there.

All conclusions, all mentations then are distilled down to a radical sense of *subjectivity*, which is the only reality that can exist. The presence of God within shines forth as Self: That Which

I Am, hmm? And that's the only thing you know, is that you exist. All the rest is software put on top of your hardware. Other than the fact that you exist, nothing else is really knowable, and all the great imaginations that all the great egos through all of time have ever arrived at—we can calibrate the Great Books of the Western World, all the greatest thinkers of all time, which I have in a library at home. These are the greatest thinkers of all time, lined up from ancient Greece; the last one of the series I think is called *Freud*, and they calibrate at 475. The greatest thinkingness in the history of the world calibrates at 475. The greatest geniuses that have ever lived, Einstein and Newton, are 499. We're looking for a reality that's in the 500s and up. So, I'm saying, don't look over here, because the world of reason and logic is not where you're going to find what you're looking for. Only the power of love can transport you, and in the nonlinear domain, it's obvious what's obvious. No proof is necessary; it would be extraneous. It would have no validity, hm? The nearest thing you can get to it from the world of logic is quantum mechanics, and the infinite quantum potentiality where you realize that consciousness alone, just by observing something—*whoosh*—totally changes its physical expression is the closest we can get to where logic and the linear and nonlinear domains meet. That's as far as reason and logic can go, is quantum mechanics, and that is the end of that box. And then you have to jump to a different paradigm. So, you realize that each of these is a different paradigm of reality. What's real in this paradigm, low on the Map, is not real in this paradigm above 200. The people in this paradigm laugh at this paradigm. "You gave all that up for love? You must be nuts. All that money, all that position, all that property, for what? For love, humph!" For love of God, that's even more outrageous.

* * *

So, reason and logic can only take us so far. It cannot really undo causality. Causality, we said—to transcend it is at about 998, or something like that. You almost have to be completely and fully enlightened to see beyond it. But to begin to doubt it, already—what we're trying to do is lessen its hold on your ego. As you begin to question it, the ego weakens. And the next session is devoted to the way of the heart. And by that time, the ego is already somewhat rickety, if you've stayed awake through any of these lectures, haha. It's become ricketized, and it falls with just a few kisses. "I love you, old ego." I said goodbye to the body a lot of times, that was sad. But saying goodbye to the mind, aww, do I have to do that? It would be sad if it was real and had a reality and it was a loss, but it's not a reality and it's not a loss; it's a gain. So, everything you let go of as far as fallacious belief systems is a freeing, a freedom.

The higher spiritual states are a way of progressive freedom, to see that the belief in causality is like a chain holding you down. You're imprisoned by a belief system. So, we're trying to weaken these belief systems and allow the butterfly within you to fly out.

Conclusion

Now that you have read this enlightening book, we hope it has cleared some of the doubts and questions you may have had about God, Spiritual Reality, and the Pathway of Nonduality.

One question that was asked in this volume is, *"How can I advance spirituality?"* Dr. Hawkins's answer, which also calibrates as a true statement, is: *"One's devotion to the truth transcends all obstacles."* This aim alone can bring great strides in a person's spiritual work.

To gain deeper insights, it is recommended to read this book often or watch or listen to the July and August 2002 lectures that are available. Dr. Hawkins tells us that just by hearing certain information can be life-altering, and through devotion, contemplation, positive choice, and dedication, a person's subjective experience can be transformed to high levels of enlightenment.

The following Spiritual statements are some of the Spiritual Truths in this book that Dr. Hawkins calibrated as correct and True:

- "God is the source and substrate of consciousness, awareness, knowingness, and sentience.
- "God is the sole source of the energy of life."
- "God is the source and essence of peace, love, stillness, and beauty."
- "God is beyond all universes, all materiality, all galaxies, and yet the source of all that is."
- "God is the ultimate context of which the universe and all that exists is the content."
- "God is the Source and essence of the subjective state of 'I-ness' called Enlightenment."

ADDITIONAL TRUTHS TO CONTEMPLATE AS YOU GO THROUGH YOUR DAY

- As we evolve spiritually, we're constantly presented with ambiguities. One way to see your way out of an ambiguity is to ask if you're mixing levels. Are you mixing levels? Things are true within a certain context. In another context, they're no longer valid.

- By Grace, each instant, everything is becoming the fulfillment of its infinite potential. Everything is manifesting the power of creation by virtue of its Source. To acknowledge God as the Source of one's existence is a very, very powerful statement, and already takes consciousness leaps ahead.

- Truth is that which brings you love and happiness, and anything else is fallacious.

- Love is a decision: "I choose to be with Thy Will, O Lord, and love unconditionally" (a prayer from Aug 2002 lecture).

- To reach the higher levels of enlightenment, intention needs to be tenacious, one-pointedness of mind, with a fixity of goal and intensity.

May the highest good be with you on your spiritual journey of awakening.

Straight and Narrow Is the Path . . . Waste No Time.

Gloria in Excelsis Deo!

About the Author

David R. Hawkins, M.D., Ph.D. (1927–2012), was director of the Institute for Spiritual Research, Inc., and founder of the Path of Devotional Nonduality. He was renowned as a pioneering researcher in the field of consciousness as well as an author, lecturer, clinician, physician, and scientist. He served as an advisor to Catholic and Protestant churches, and Buddhist monasteries; appeared on major network television and radio programs; and lectured widely at such places as Westminster Abbey, the Oxford Forum, the University of Notre Dame, and Harvard University. His life was devoted to the upliftment of mankind until his death in 2012.

For more information on Dr. Hawkins's work, visit
veritaspub.com

Hay House Titles of Related Interest

YOU CAN HEAL YOUR LIFE, the movie,
starring Louise Hay & Friends
(available as an online streaming video)
www.hayhouse.co.uk/louise-movie

THE SHIFT, the movie,
starring Dr. Wayne W. Dyer
(available as an online streaming video)
www.hayhouse.co.uk/the-shift-movie

***

PURE HUMAN: The Hidden Truth of Our Divinity, Power, and Destiny by Gregg Braden

THE WISDOM OF THE COUNCIL: Channeled Messages for Living Your Purpose by Sara Landon

ANSWERS FROM THE ANCESTRAL REALMS: Get Psychic Help from Your Spirit Guides Every Day by Sharon Anne Klinger

DIRECTING OUR INNER LIGHT: Using Meditation to Heal the Body, Mind, and Spirit by Brian L. Weiss, M.D.

All of the above are available at your local bookstore,
or may be ordered by contacting Hay House (see next page).

***

We hope you enjoyed this Hay House book. If you'd like to receive our online catalogue featuring additional information on Hay House books and products, please contact:

Hay House UK Ltd
1st Floor, Crawford Corner,
91–93 Baker Street, London W1U 6QQ
Tel: +44 (0)20 3927 7290; www.hayhouse.co.uk

Published in the United States of America by:
Hay House LLC
PO Box 5100, Carlsbad, CA 92018-5100
Tel: (760) 431-7695 or (800) 654-5126
www.hayhouse.com

Published in Australia by:
Hay House Australia Publishing Pty Ltd
18/36 Ralph St., Alexandria NSW 2015
Tel: +61 (02) 9669 4299
www.hayhouse.com.au

Published in India by:
Hay House Publishers (India) Pvt Ltd
Muskaan Complex, Plot No. 3,
B-2, Vasant Kunj, New Delhi 110 070
Tel: +91 11 41761620
www.hayhouse.co.in

Let Your Soul Grow

Experience life-changing transformation – one video at a time – with guidance from the world's leading experts.

www.healyourlifeplus.com

TRANSFORM YOUR DAY— ANYTIME, ANYWHERE

With the **Empower You** Unlimited Audio *App*

66 ★★★★★ **Life changing.**
My fav app on my entire phone, hands down! – Gigi 99

Unlimited access to the entire Hay House audio library!

You'll get:

- 600+ soul-stirring **audiobooks** to expand your mind
- 1,000+ **meditations** for restful sleep, morning focus, and gentle healing
- Bite-sized audios **under 20 minutes**—perfect for busy days
- **Exclusive talks** you won't find anywhere else
- Daily affirmations
- Fresh content added **every week** to fuel your journey

New audios added every week!

66 Driving, yard work, and housework have been **transformed**!
– Ruffles27 99

Scan the QR code to start listening or visit **hayhouse.com/unlimited**

HAY HOUSE
Online Video Courses

Your journey to a better life starts with figuring out which path is best for you. Hay House Online Courses provide guidance in mental and physical health, personal finance, telling your unique story, and so much more!

LEARN HOW TO:

- choose your words and actions wisely so you can tap into life's magic
- clear the energy in yourself and your environments for improved clarity, peace, and joy
- forgive, visualize, and trust in order to create a life of authenticity and abundance
- manifest lifelong health by improving nutrition, reducing stress, improving sleep, and more
- create your own unique angelic communication toolkit to help you to receive clear messages for yourself and others
- use the creative power of the quantum realm to create health and well-being

To find the guide for your journey, visit www.HayHouseU.com.

HAY HOUSE
online learning

CONNECT WITH
HAY HOUSE
ONLINE

🌐 hayhouse.co.uk   f @hayhouse

📷 @hayhouseuk   🦋 @hayhouseuk.bsky.social

🎵 @hayhouseuk   ▶ @HayHousePresents

Find out all about our latest books & card decks • Be the first to know about exclusive discounts • Interact with our authors in live broadcasts • Celebrate the cycle of the seasons with us • Watch free videos from your favourite authors • Connect with like-minded souls

---

'The gateways to wisdom and knowledge are always open.'

Louise Hay